A Little Taste of Jamaica

Andrea Walters

Laura I hope you find pleasure
preparing each meal!
Enjoy! God bless you richly.
Andrea Walters

AuthorHouse™
1663 Liberty Drive
Bloomington, IN 47403
www.authorhouse.com
Phone: 1-800-839-8640

First published by AuthorHouse 3/9/2011

ISBN: 978-1-4567-1416-1 (sc)

Library of Congress Control Number: 2010918956

Printed in the United States of America

Any people depicted in stock imagery provided by Thinkstock are models, and such images are being used for illustrative purposes only. Certain stock imagery © Thinkstock.

This book is printed on acid-free paper.

authorHOUSE®

Acknowledgement

I give thanks to the Almighty God for strength, vision, knowledge, wisdom and perseverance in enabling me to write this book.

Thank you to my husband, Everton, for supporting me and cooking up mouth watering meals worthy of pictures.

Thanks to my daughter Raecine, who assisted in typing from the hard copies I prepared when my thoughts flowed.

Thanks to my sons Craig, and starry-eyed Ryan, for believing and supporting me.

Thanks to my mother, Doris Walters, who along with my dad (now deceased), gave me an education. Thank you for being my mother. It's not easy. You never gave up. You are an inspiration.

Thanks to my friends who believed in my ability, prayed for me, and inspired me through words like this "you can do it, keep going, one recipe at a time".

Thanks to my niece Stacey and sister Dione for their help.

Thanks to my co-workers who inspired me to insert pictures in this book and to finish it.

Thanks to all my fans. "You have inspired and encouraged me. Some of you even gave me your telephone numbers, "saying here's my number, call me when this book is finish." Thank you for your trust and vote of confidence.

Thanks to you all – I give you, "A LITTLE TASTE OF JAMAICA."

Table of Contents

About This Book   viii
Did You Know That   ix
About The Author   x

Entrees

French Fried Chicken   2
Chicken Gravy   4
Rice and Peas   5
Stew Peas and White Rice   7
White Rice   9
Jerk Chicken   10
Curry Goat   12
Oxtail and Beans   14
Curry Chicken   16
Bake Chicken   18
Roast Chicken   20
Barbeque/Grilled Chicken   21
Barbeque Sauce   22
Buffalo Chicken Wings   23
Fricasee Chicken   24
Stew Chicken   25
Chicken Chop Suey or Chicken Stir Fry   27
Shake & Bake Chicken   29
Stewed Chicken Feet   30
Sweet & Sour Chicken   31
Steamed Fish   32
White Soft Yam, Pumpkin, Green Bananas & Dumplings   33
Escovitch Fish   35
Brown Stew Fish   37
Fried Fish   39
Bake Fish   41
Stew Pork   42
Pork Chops   43
Shake & Baked Pork Chops   45
Barbeque Spare Ribs   46
Barbeque Pork Chops   47
Jerk Pork   48
Pig Trotters (Pig Feet)   49
Tripe & Beans   50

Stew Beef	51
Peppered Steak	52
Cow Foot and Beans	53
Cow Skin And Beans	54
Pot Roast Beef	55
Baked Jacketed Potatoes	56
Corned Beef & Cabbage	57
Salt Fish & Cabbage	58
Cabbage & (Mince) Ground Beef	59
Meat Balls	60
Corned Beef & Spaghetti/Macaroni)	61
Corned Beef & Rice	62
Macaroni & Saltfish Stew	63
Okra & Saltfish Stew	64
Saltfish Stew	66
Butter Bean & Saltfish	68
Ackee & Saltfish	70
Ackee & Red Herring	72
Red Peas Soup	73
Guango Peas (Pigeon) Soup	75
Chicken Feet/Vegetable Soup	77
Fish Tea Soup	79
Goat Head Soup or (Manish Water)	81
Pepper-Pot Soup	83
Beef Soup	85
Green Guango & Saltfish Stew	87
Susumber, Ackee & Saltfish Stew	88
Kidney And Green Bananas	89
(Pickled) Salt Mackerel With Dumpling & Green Bananas	90
Mackerel & Run Down	92
Festival	93
Fried Dumplings (Johnny Cake)	94
Saltfish Fritters	96
Fried Breadfruit	97
Bammy	98
Fried Plantains	99
Fried Green Bananas/Plantain	100
Liver, Bacon, Onions & Green Bananas	101
Turn Cornmeal	103
Steamed Callaloo	104
Pumpkin & Rice	106
Seasoned Rice	107
Tin (Canned) Mackerel with Dumplings and Green Bananas	109

Breakfast

Roast Breadfruit	112
Chocolate Tea	113
Scrambled Eggs	115

Salads

Potato Salad	118
Macaroni Salad	119
Tossed Salad	121

Juices

Soursop Juice	124
Carrot Juice	125
Carrot & Beet Root Juice	126
Beet Root Juice	127
June Plum Juice	128
Cucumber Juice	129
Cucumber & Melon Drink	130
Ginger Ale	131
Passion Fruit	132
Papaya Juice	133
Fruit Punch	134
Pineapple Juice	135

Snacks

Coconut or Cut Cake	138
Coconut Grated Cake	139
Rock Bun	140
Sweet Potato Pudding	141
Cornmeal Pudding	142
Bread Pudding	143
Christmas Cake / Wedding Cake Or (Black Cake)	144
Pineapple Up-Side Down Cake	146

Cornmeal Porridge   148
Cream of Wheat Porridge   149
Oats Porridge   150
Plantain Porridge   151
Green Banana Porridge   152
Rice Porridge   153
Bulga Porridge   154
Hominy Corn Porridge   155

"How To"- Tid Bits   156

About This Book

"A Little Taste of Jamaica" is a creation of Jamaican recipes put together as a 'gift' from the author to her culture and homeland - Jamaica.

Its primary purpose is to help preserve the "Jamaican Culture"

I have found out while living here in the United States of America, that there are many Jamaican families whose parents, grand parents, aunts or uncles know how to cook Jamaican food, but their children or grand children have not inherited any culinary skills. They long to cook like their parents, but have not been taught.

Another purpose of this book is to preserve and pass on the culture, the recipes, and a taste of the "Jamaican Food".

Many restaurants and cooks would love to cook "Jamaican Style", and some have tried and have fallen short.

Jamaica has developed a popularity for certain of its foods. People of different nationality have tasted, and desire to taste again or even prepare this food.

I give you "A little taste of Jamaica". Allow it to impart knowledge through its recipes, giving a fresh perspective on cooking "Jamaican Style Food".

Open its pages! ....enjoy Jamaican Jerk Chicken, Oxtail, Curry Chicken and more!!
mmmh! mouth-watering!

Did You Know That

1. Jamaica is an island located in the West Indies. It is surrounded by the Caribbean Sea; hence its location, in the Caribbean.

2. Jamaica's closest neighbors are Cuba, Haiti, Dominican Republic and Florida.

3. Jamaica is approximately 1,044 square miles. It has 14 parishes and 3 counties.

4. Reggae music originated out of Jamaica.

5. "Jerk"- a type of cooking originated out of Jamaica from which we have the popular jerk chicken, jerk pork,

6. Jamaica's national dish is "Ackee and Saltfish".

7. Jamaica's folklore culture was made popular by the late Louise Bennett Coverley.

8. Jamaicans speak a language called "Patois", indigenous to the island.
   (Mi nuh khare) interpreted (I don't care).

9. Jamaica's official language is English.

10. Jamaica gained their independence from England on August 6, 1962.

11. Tourism plays a vital role in the Jamaican economy, and it's the home of white sand beaches, crystal clear water, and the renowned "Dunns River Falls in Ochio Rios.

About The Author

The author, Andrea Walters was born in Gordon Town, St. Andrew, Jamaica in a small district called Dublin Castle. She attended the local school – St. Martin dePores Primary, and later Jones Town Primary, where she was successful in the then, Common Entrance Exam; and took a transfer to Excelsior High School.

Andrea hails from a large family, who during her early years moved to Cooper's Ridge District where her parents settled down amongst relatives and friends and grew their children.

She is the fifth of eleven children, and like most Jamaicans (who are born chefs); she began cooking at the age of twelve (12). She recalls that each sibling had their share of the kitchen, and some as early as eight (8) years of age.

Andrea is a woman of faith, and gives praise to her God, the Lord Jesus Christ for vision and wisdom in enabling her to write this book.

She also gives credit to her Alma Mater – Excelsior High School for awakening her culinary skills; as Food & Nutrition was one of her subjects studied and passed.

Andrea is married to Everton Grant. She has three (3) children. Craig, Raecine and Ryan.

She was a Secretary in Corporate Jamaica for several years. She later migrated to the United States, where she still takes pleasure in preparing delectable meals for her family and special functions.

Entrees

French Fried Chicken

<u>Ingredients:</u>
2 lbs chicken
2 tbsp vinegar (white)
2 eggs
1 cup vegetable cooking oil/olive oil
¼ tsp salt
1 small onion
1 sprig thyme
1 stalk eskellion or green onion
½ tsp season all/old bay seasoning
pinch scotch bonnet pepper
1 cup all-purpose flour.
1 clove garlic
2-4 seeds crushed pimento
1 tbsp soy sauce or Chinese sauce
¼ tsp baking powder (optional)

<u>Method</u>
1. Clean and cut chicken in desired pieces.
2. Place chicken in pan, add vinegar and water and rinse chicken.
3. Do not remove chicken skin. Drain.
4. Chop or grate eskellion, onion and garlic and add all seasonings including powder/ dry seasonings.
5. Rub seasoning into chicken, cover and leave to marinate between 10-30 minutes.
6. Break eggs in a bowl, remove "eye of the egg" and beat or whisk eggs as if to prepare scramble eggs.
7. Place flour in a bowl. Add a pinch of salt, baking powder, black pepper, all purpose, old bay or all powder seasonings.
8. Mix seasonings and flour together.
9. Heat frying pan/deep fat fryer and add vegetable cooking oil.
10. Scrape seasonings of the chicken, then dip chicken in egg batter, then roll it in seasoned flour.
11. Shake off excess flour and place in hot oil.
12. Adjust heat so that chicken is fried slowly to a golden brown color, turning it over from side to side as necessary.
13. When fully cooked and golden brown, place chicken on a napkin in plate or basket to drain off excess oil.
14. Remove flaking deposited in the oil from time to time to prevent burning of chicken or the flaking attaching itself to the chicken.

* Crushed Corn flakes or bread crumbs can be substituted for flour.

Serves 4
Enjoy with a delicious plate of rice and peas and your favorite juice!

French Fried Chicken

Chicken Gravy

<u>Ingredients:</u>

1. All seasonings remaining in bowl from fried chicken
2. 1 tbsp browning/soya sauce.
3. 1 tbsp ketchup
4. 1 cup cold water
5. 1 tsp corn starch for thickening (optional)
6. 1 tbsp sugar
7. 1 tbsp red wine (optional)
8. 1 dash of old bay seasoning/or dried seasoning
9. 1 dash of black pepper

<u>Method:</u>

1. Heat sauce pan and add 1 tbsp oil from the pan the chicken was fried in.
2. Add seasonings from sauce pan.
3. Add cup of cold water.
4. Stir, and add all other ingredients except corn starch.
5. Stir, lower flame cover and bring to a boil.
6. Add corn starch to a cup or small container, add a little water and mix to a smooth paste. Add to the mixture in pot. Stir.
7. Allow to simmer for approximately 5 minutes. Season to taste.

Enjoy along with your fried chicken or favorite menu!

Rice and Peas

<u>Ingredients:</u>

1 canned coconut milk
1 uncut scotch bonnet pepper for flavoring
1 tsp salt
black pepper
2-4 seeds pimento
1 stalk eskellion/green onion
1 clove garlic
1 pack red kidney beans
1 tsp sugar (optional)
2 lbs rice (brown optional)
1 sprig thyme
Powder seasonings

<u>Method</u>

1. Rinse peas and place in a pot with enough water to cover the peas.
2. Peel and slightly crush garlic and add to peas.
3. Cover and leave peas to soak overnight or for at least 30-40 minutes. The peas should absorb the water and begin to split open.
4. Add approximately 1 cup water to peas, cover and place on fire.
5. Open can of coconut milk and add to peas, filling the empty can with cold tap water at least 3 times, pouring on peas.
6. Allow coconut and peas to cook for approximately 40 minutes until peas is soft and tender to touch and coconut cream rises to the top of mixture.
7. Add salt. Black pepper, pimento, sugar, scotch bonnet pepper, eskellion, thyme, and powder seasonings. Stir cover and allow seasonings to cook for another 10 minutes.
8. Rinse rice, drain and add to mixture. Stir and lower flame; allow to cook until rice is dried and flakes are tender.

*As soon as rice begins to dry or rice is place in pot, the pot can be placed in a hot oven at 300-350°F. This takes the "quess" out of when the rice is cooked and also prevents the rice from being easily burnt

Serves 8 ENJOY!!

Rice and Peas

Stew Peas and White Rice

Ingredients:

1 red kidney beans
½-1 lbs salt beef
½-1lbs pigs tail
1 lbs fresh beef (optional)
small piece of ginger
¼ lbs flour
1 clove garlic
2 stalk eskellion (green onion)
1 sprig thyme
1 cup coconut milk (optional)
Dry or powdered seasonings as desired.
1 uncut scotch bonnet pepper
4-6 seeds pimento

Method

1. Rinse kidney beans in desired pot for cooking. Add enough water to cover the beans. Peel and crush garlic in pot cover and leave the beans/peas to soak until tender, preferable overnight.

2. Rinse and cut pigs tail and salt beef in separate container. Place enough water to immerse. Cover and leave to soak, in refrigerator, preferably overnight to remove excess salt.

3. Clean, chop beef in small pieces season and leave to marinate for approximately 20 minutes.

4. Place pot with kidney beans/red peas on stove to cook. Add 2 cups of water as the peas would have absorbed all the water it was soaking in. (If the peas was not soaking, rinse it place in pot, add clove of garlic and add just enough water to cover peas. Bring to boil, then add 3-4 cups of water to sink the peas.)

5. Add the coconut milk, gently crush ginger stir and leave to cook. Do not seal the pot cover to prevent the mixture from running over the sides of the pot.

6. Remove pigs tail and salt beef from refrigerator. Throw off the water then add fresh water. Place in a pot of water to boil or scald for 5-10 minutes to remove excess salt.

7. Add pigs tail salt beef to the peas pot stir and allow mixture to cook until tender.

8. While peas is cooking, heat sauce pan, add beef, rinse pan with a little water and add to sauce

pan. Stir and cover. Allow beef to brown and cook at the same time until tender. When complete beef should be brown and has a little gravy ready to eat.

9. Check peas/meat with a fork for tenderness. The coconut cream should rise to the top of the mixture. If it attaches to the side of the pot scrape off with a spoon and allow it to fall into the mixture.

10. Add the beef mixture along with gravy. Stir.

11. Add flour to a clean bowl, add a pinch of salt and a tbsp of cornmeal (optional). Stir. Place water, approximately 3 tbsp of water in flour mixture. Mix and knead the mixture to the right consistency. It should not be hard or soft. Roll mixture between the palms of your hands to make small dumplings called "Spinners" or "Wheely Tongue" dumplings, and add to the pot.

12. Rinse pepper, thyme and eskellion under tap. Crush eskellion gently and add to pot with pepper, thyme , pimentos and any dry seasonings. DO NOT ADD SALT.

13. Stir, cover and allow to simmer for approximately 10-15 minutes on low heat to allow dumplings to cook.

14. Serve with white rice.

P.S Stew peas can be cooked with a variety of peas and meat such as chicken, smoked turkey, turkey/ turkey neck etc. The chicken would be prepared and cook just like the beef then added. If smoked turkey is used it would just be added to the mixture while the peas is cooking as it is pre cooked.

Enjoy!
Serves 6-8

White Rice

<u>Ingredients:</u>

2 cup white or brown rice
¼-1/2 tsp salt
½ tbsp butter (optional)

<u>Method:</u>

1. Place rice in a small pot .
2. Add 3 cups water, add salt stir, cover and bring to boil on low heat.
3. Adjust flame to its lowest when rice starts drying. Cover and leave rice to cook until dry and tender, or remove pot from flame and place in an oven at 300-350°F and allow to cook until dry and tender for 10-20 minutes.

Serve with your favorite Side dish!

Jerk Chicken

<u>Ingredients:</u>

2-3 lbs chicken
1 onion
1 clove chopped garlic
1 pinch scotch bonnet pepper
4-6 seeds pimento
1 stalk eskellion/green onion
1 sprig thyme
1 sprig cilantro
1 sprig basil
1 tbsp browning
¼-1/2 tsp salt
2-3 tbsp Hot Grace Jerk Seasoning (Mild flavor can be used but would require more seasoning).
6-8 sliced pieces bell pepper/sweet pepper of different colors (optional)

<u>Method:</u>

1. Clean chicken removing skin, rinse in vinegar water and cut in small pieces.
2. Peel and slice onion, peel and chop eskellion, and chop basil and cilantro.
3. Place seasonings in food processor and chop finely. Remove and add all seasonings/spices along with Jerk seasoning to chicken in a clean bowl. Use a disposable gloves to rub all seasonings together and leave to marinate for approximately 30-60 minutes.
4. Heat oven to 350º. Place chicken in casserole dish/baking pan, cover with foil for the 1st 15 minutes of baking and place on 2nd rack in oven and bake.
5. Remove foil and allow chicken to bake until tender. Base chicken with juices extracted from chicken at the bottom of the casserole/baking pan.
6. Garnish with bell pepper slices or parsley and serve with your favorite side order.

PS

Chicken can be done on a barbecue grill.

Enjoy!

Serves 4-6

Jerk Chicken

Curry Goat

Ingredients:

2-3 lbs goat meat
1 onion
2 cloves chopped garlic
1 pinch scotch bonnet pepper
1 uncut scotch bonnet pepper
4-6 seeds pimento
1 stalk eskellion/green onion
1 sprig thyme
1 sprig cilantro
1 sprig basil
¼-1/2 tsp salt
few diced/sliced pieces bell pepper/sweet pepper of different colors
2-3 tbsp curry powder
Dash of All purpose seasoning/dry seasonings
1 small potato (optional)

Method:

1. Clean goat meat removing excess fat, rinse meat in vinegar water and cut in small pieces, or can be purchased, cut in desired cooking size.
2. Peel and slice onion, peel and chop eskellion, and chop basil and cilantro and add all spices to goat in a clean bowl. Use disposable gloves to rub all seasonings together and leave to marinate for approximately 30-60 minutes or even overnight.
3. Heat saucepan/pot and add goat meat. Do not use any oil. Swiss bowl with a little water to remove all seasoning and pour it unto the goat. Stir. Cover, and cook on medium flame until tender, stirring frequently.
4. It should be noted that if goat is cooking for approximately 1 hour, and meat is not tender then contents of pot can be transferred to a pressure cooker and meat pressured for approximately 10-20 minutes or until tender.

5. When goat is tender, peel and diced potatoes into small cubes. Rinse and add to the goat. Stir and leave to cook. Goat will give off water while cooking but if necessary add a little water at a time to prevent burning or meat sticking to the bottom of the pot.
6. Re-season the pot to taste, add uncut pepper, lower flame, and simmer for approximately 10 minutes.

PS: The longer meat is left to marinate the more flavorful it is.

Enjoy!

Serves 4-6

Curry Goat

Oxtail and Beans

Ingredients:
2-3 lbs oxtail
1 onion
2 cloves chopped garlic
1 pinch scotch bonnet pepper
1 uncut scotch bonnet pepper
4-6 seeds pimento
1 stalk eskellion/green onion
1 sprig thyme
1 sprig cilantro
1 sprig basil
¼-1/2 tsp salt
few diced/sliced pieces bell pepper/sweet pepper of different colors
Dash of All purpose seasoning/dry seasonings
1 tbsp soya sauce
1 tbsp browning
1 tbsp vegetable cooking oil
1 pack lima bean or 1 can grace butter bean

Method:

1. Clean oxtail removing excess fat, rinse meat in vinegar water. This meat is usually bought in the size ready to cook.
2. Peel and slice onion, peel and chop eskellion, and chop basil and cilantro and add all spices to oxtail in a clean bowl. Use a disposable gloves to rub all seasonings together and leave to marinate for approximately 30-60 minutes or even overnight.
3. Heat saucepan, add vegetable oil and heat. Use a fork to remove the seasonings from the meat and add oxtail to sauce pan. Stir, cover and allow to meat to fry until brown. Cover seasonings and put it aside.
4. Rinse lima beans if used, and leave to soak with a clove of garlic. This can be cooked separately and added to the oxtail or better still cooked with the oxtail for added flavor.
5. After oxtail is browned or fried, transfer to a pot. Add the seasoning from the bowl. Add a little water to the bowl to remove all seasonings and add to pot. Add lima beans and contents. Add a cup of water to ensure that meat has adequate amount of water.
6. Cook on medium flame for approximately 1 hour stirring frequently until meat is tender and loosening from the bone. Or, transfer contents to a pressure cooker and pressure for approximately 30 minutes or until meat is tender.
7. Re-season the pot to taste, add uncut pepper, lower flame, canned butter bean if used. Simmer for approximately 10 minutes.

PS: The longer meat is left to marinate the more flavorful it is.

Enjoy!

Serves 6-8

Oxtail and Beans

Curry Chicken

Ingredients:

2-3 lbs chicken
1 onion
2 cloves chopped garlic
1 pinch scotch bonnet pepper
1 uncut scotch bonnet pepper
4-6 seeds pimento
1 stalk eskellion/green onion
1 sprig thyme
1 sprig cilantro
1 sprig basil
¼-1/2 tsp salt
few diced/sliced pieces bell pepper/sweet pepper of different colors
2-3 tbsp curry powder
1 tsp olive/vegetable oil
Dash of All purpose seasoning/dry seasonings
1 small potato (optional)

Method:

1. Clean chicken removing skin, rinse in vinegar water and cut in small pieces.
2. Peel and slice onion, peel and chop eskellion, and chop basil and cilantro and add all spices to chicken in a clean bowl.
3. Add olive/vegetable oil to bowl. Use a disposable gloves to rub all seasonings together and leave to marinate for approximately 30-60 minutes or even overnight.
4. Heat saucepan and add chicken. Swiss bowl with a little water to remove all seasonings and add it to the chicken. Stir.
5. Cover, and cook over medium flame, stirring frequently. Do not allow chicken to fry or stick to pot or burn. While covered, chicken will give off steam enabling it to cook. If necessary, while stirring frequently, add a little water.
6. Approximately 5 minutes before chicken is fully cooked, peel and diced potatoes into small cubes, and add to the pot.
7. Re-season the chicken to taste, add uncut scotch-bonnet pepper, lower flame, and simmer for approximately 5-10 minutes, and serve with your favorite side order.

PS: The longer meat/chicken is left to marinate the more flavorful it is.

Enjoy!
Serves 4-6

Curry Chicken

Bake Chicken

<u>Ingredients:</u>

2-3 lbs chicken
1 onion
2 cloves chopped garlic
4-6 seeds pimento
1 stalk eskellion/green onion
1 sprig thyme
1 sprig cilantro
1 sprig basil
¼-1/2 tsp salt
Dash of All purpose seasoning/dry seasonings
Aluminum Foil

<u>Method:</u>

1. Clean chicken removing skin, rinse in vinegar water and cut in regular joints as desired.
2. Peel and slice onion, eskellion, basil and cilantro. Add all spices and herbs to chicken in a clean bowl.
3. Use a disposable gloves to rub all seasonings together and leave to marinate for approximately 30-60 minutes or even overnight.
4. Heat oven to 375 degree. Place chicken in casserole dish/baking pan, making sure that all seasoning is placed on the bottom of the pan like a bed of flowers and chicken is placed on top. Make sure no seasoning is on top of chicken. This is done so that the herbs and spices will add flavor as chicken is baked, without getting burnt first.
5. Cover /seal with foil and place on 2nd rack in oven. Bake for 30-40 minutes remove foil.
6. Continue to bake for another 20-30 minutes basting chicken with juices extracted from the chicken while it was covered. Turn chicken unto other side half way into baking time and baste.
7. At the end of baking time chicken should be tender and baked with light brown color. Chicken will also make its own gravy.
8. Remove from oven and serve with your favorite side order.

PS: It should be noted that the longer meat is left to marinate the more flavorful it is

Enjoy!
Serves 4-6

Bake Chicken

Roast Chicken

<u>Ingredients:</u>

1 medium-large roasting chicken
½ tsp salt
Dash black pepper
Dash powdered seasonings
2 tbsp vinegar
4-6 crushed pimento
1 large onion
2 cloves garlic
Piece of ginger

<u>Method:</u>

1. Clean chicken, by cutting off excess fat at the opening of the chicken insides, cut off tail and clean out the chicken insides. All liver should be cleaned out of the back of the chicken.
2. Place chicken in a bowl of water, add vinegar and rinse.
3. Drain and place chicken on cutting board.
4. Grate or puree ginger, garlic and onion and place in a small bowl. Add pimentos.
5. Add powdered seasonings to chicken, particularly, the inside of the chicken. Add the seasonings in the bowl all over the chicken.
6. Use a glove to rub the seasonings into the chicken. Leave to marinate for approximately 30 minutes.
7. Heat oven to 375 degrees, place in baking dish, cover with aluminum foil, set oven timer for 30 minutes and bake.
8. Remove foil and continue baking chicken.
9. Baste chicken with fluid in baking dish drained from chicken.
10. Bake until golden brown and tender.
11. Remove from oven, place on a platter, garnish with parsley and serve with your favorite side dish

Serves 4-6
Enjoy!

Barbeque/Grilled Chicken

<u>Ingredients:</u>

2-3 lbs chicken
1 onion
1 clove chopped garlic
1 pinch scotch bonnet pepper
4-6 seeds pimento
1 stalk eskellion/green onion
1 sprig thyme
1 sprig cilantro
1 sprig basil
¼-1/2 tsp salt
Dash of powder seasonings

<u>Method:</u>

1. Clean chicken removing skin, rinse in vinegar water and cut in desired pieces.
2. Peel and slice onion, peel and chop eskellion, and chop basil and cilantro.
3. Add all seasonings to chicken in a clean bowl. Use a disposable gloves to rub all seasonings together and leave to marinate for approximately 30-60 minutes.
4. Heat oven to 350°, or light and heat portable grill. Place chicken in casserole dish/baking pan. Use a fork to remove herbal seasonings off the top of chicken as this burn first. Place the herbs on the base of the baking dish as a bed and place chicken on top of herbs. (Chicken will extract flavor as it bake if casserole dish/pan is used)
5. Cover with foil for the 1st 15 minutes of baking and place on 2nd rack in oven.
6. Remove foil and allow chicken to bake until tender. Base chicken with barbeque sauce and or juices extracted from chicken and bake until tender.
7. Turn chicken unto other side base, and allow heat to penetrate for another 5-10 minutes.
8. Garnish with parsley and serve with your favorite side order.

PS Chicken can be done on a barbecue grill.

BARBEQUE SAUCE SHOULD NOT BE USED FOR GRILLED CHICKEN , USE JUICES EXTRACTED FROM CHICKEN WHILE BAKING TO BASE AND ALSO MAKE A SAUCE FOR GRILLED CHICKEN

Barbeque Sauce

<u>Ingredients</u>

2 tbsp lime juice
dash cinnamon
dash of nutmeg
pinch of salt
pinch of black pepper
2 tbsp white vinegar
2 tbsp sugar
2 tbsp honey (optional)
1 tsp cornstarch (optional)
¼ cup ketchup
¼ cup kraft barbeque sauce

Method:

1. Mix all spices and seasonings in a sauce pot.
2. Bring to boil over low flame mixing the corn starch in a little water and adding to the mixture to thicken if necessary.
3. Remove from flame. Base chicken in oven.

Enjoy!
Serves 4-6

Buffalo Chicken Wings

Ingredients:

2-3 lbs chicken wings
1 onion
1 clove chopped garlic
1 pinch scotch bonnet pepper
4-6 seeds pimento
1 stalk eskellion/green onion
1 sprig thyme
1 sprig cilantro
1 sprig basil
¼-1/2 tsp salt
Dash of powder seasonings
2 tbsp lime juice
Pinch cinnamon
2 tbsp vinegar
2 tbsp sugar
1 bottle Honey Smoked Barbeque Sauce
2-4 tbsp ketchup
1 tsp cornstrch

Method:

1. Clean chicken, rinse in vinegar water and cut in desired pieces.
2. Peel and slice onion, peel and chop eskellion, and chop basil and cilantro.
3. Add all seasonings to chicken in a clean bowl. Use disposable gloves to rub all seasonings together and leave to marinate for approximately 30-60 minutes.
4. Place 1-2 cups of water in a large saucepan, enough just to cover chicken.
5. Add chicken wings along with seasonings. Cover and boil for approximately 10 minutes. Turn off flame drain stock and put aside.
6. Heat oven to 350°F, remove chicken from pot, and place in baking dish.
7. Pour stock in a small bowl or pot. Add lime juice, cinnamon, vinegar, sugar, ½ bottle Kraft honey hickory Smoked barbeque sauce and tomato ketchup. Stir. Mix cornstarch and add. Bring to a quick boil and allow to thicken.
8. Base chicken and place in oven. Bake for 25-30 minutes until tender. Turn from side to side basting as chicken is baked.
9. Garnish with parsley and serve with your favorite side order.

Fricasee Chicken

<u>Ingredients:</u>

2 lbs chicken
2 tbsp vinegar (white)
½ cup vegetable cooking oil
¼ tsp salt
1 small onion
1 sprig thyme
1 stalk eskellion or green onion
½ tsp season all/old bay seasoning
pinch scotch bonnet pepper
1 clove garlic
2-4 seeds crushed pimento
1 tbsp soy sauce or Chinese sauce
1 tbsp browning
1 tbsp ketchup (optional)
1 tsp cornstarch (optional)

<u>Method</u>

1. Clean and cut chicken in desired pieces.
2. Place chicken in pan, add vinegar and water and rinse chicken.
3. Chop or grate eskellion, onion and garlic and add all seasonings including powder/dry seasonings, allow to marinate 10-15 minutes.
4. Heat pan/deep fat fryer and add vegetable cooking oil
5. Scrape seasonings of the chicken using a fork or knife, and place in hot oil to fry until brown. Remove and place in pan with seasoning, keep covered.
6. Remove excess oil leaving approx 1-2 tbsp. Add fry chicken along with all seasonings in pan. Add 2 cups water to seasoning bowl, swiss around seasonings and add to chicken. Stir.
7. Adjust to low flame, add a dash of onion, herbs and spices, ketchup, browning and or soya sauce.
8. Mix 1tsp cornstarch in 2-4 tsps water and add to chicken to thicken if necessary.
9. Cover and allow chicken to cook/simmer for approximately 10-12 minutes.
10. Stir.

Serve 4-6
Enjoy with your favorite side dish!

Stew Chicken

<u>Ingredients:</u>

2 lbs chicken
2 tbsp vinegar (white)
¼ tsp salt
1 small onion
1 sprig thyme
1 stalk eskellion or green onion
½ tsp season all/old bay seasoning
pinch scotch bonnet pepper
1 clove garlic
2-4 seeds crushed pimento
1 tbsp soy sauce or Chinese sauce
1 tbsp browning
1/2 bell pepper (assorted colors)

<u>Method</u>
1. Clean and cut chicken in desired pieces.
2. Place chicken in pan, add vinegar and water and rinse chicken.
3. Chop or grate eskellion, onion and garlic and add all seasonings including powder/dry seasonings.
4. Rub in all seasonings and leave to marinate for approx. 10-20 minutes.
5. Heat saucepan and add seasoned chicken. Swiss pan with a little water to remove all seasonings and add to the sauce pan. Stir and cover.
6. Lower flame, stir occasionally, keep covered, and allow chicken to cook and brown for approximately 30 minutes until tender.
7. Chicken will make its own gravy. Add a tbsp ketchup if desired.
8. Reseason with onion and a dash of spices if necessary.
9. Stir, remove from flame. Serve with your favorite side order.

Serve 4-6
Enjoy with your favorite side dish!

Stew Chicken

Chicken Chop Suey or Chicken Stir Fry

<u>Ingredients:</u>

2 lbs chicken
2 tbsp vinegar (white)
¼ tsp salt
1 tbsp olive oil
1 large onion
1 sprig thyme
2-3 stalk eskellion or green onion
½ tsp season all/old bay seasoning
pinch scotch bonnet pepper
2 clove garlic
2-4 seeds crushed pimento
1-2 tbsp soy sauce or Chinese sauce
1 bottle stir fry sauce
1/2 bell pepper (assorted colors)
2 lbs/bunches pak choy
2-4 medium carrots
1 small squash
1 small zucchini
Few sprigs of basil, parsley, cilantro
1 pk or can mixed vegetables (drained)
1 pk or canned corn (drained)
*A pack or 2 of stir fry can be used to substitute for fresh vegetables.
*Shrimp and beef can be used for this stir fry combined or separately.

<u>Method</u>

1. Clean and cut chicken in desired pieces.
2. Place chicken in pan, add vinegar and water and rinse chicken.
3. Chop or grate 1 eskellion, ½ of onion, and 1 clove garlic. Add all seasonings including powder/ dry seasonings.
4. Rub in all seasonings and leave to marinate for approx. 10-20 minutes.
5. Heat saucepan and add seasoned chicken. Rinse pan with a little water and add to the
6. sauce pan. Stir and cover.
7. Rinse all vegetables in vinegar water and set aside in colander to drain.
8. Peel carrots and cut along with bell peppers cut in thin strips. Zucchini, cucumber and squash cut in 3/4inch cubes. Slice onion, chop basil and or parsley, garlic basil, and eskellion.   C u t the pak choy in measurements of approximately 1 inch.
9. Lower flame, stir occasionally, keep covered, and allow chicken to cook and brown for approximately 10-15 minutes until tender. Then remove from flame.

10. Heat a large sauce pan and add the olive oil. Add all the vegetables, herbs, oninons, garlic eskellion, bell peppers and sauté for approx. 3 minutes stirring constantly.
11. Cover pot, lower flame for approx. 2 minutes.
12. Add chicken and gravy, Stir.
13. Add 2 tbsp stir fry sauce, 1-2 tbsp soy sauce/chinese and a dash of powdered seasonings to flavor.
14. Stir, cover sauce pan and allow to simmer for appprox 3-5 minutes.
15. Stir, remove from flame.

Serve 4-6
Enjoy with your favorite side dish!

Shake & Bake Chicken

Ingredients:

2 lbs chicken
4-8 pimento seeds (crushed)
1 sprig thyme
1 sprig basil (optional)
1 sprig cilantro (optional)
2 cloves garlic (chopped)
1/3 tsp salt
1 small onion sliced
1 pk shake & bake chicken or
1-2 cups bread crumbs or corn flakes
Dash old bay seasoning
Dash blackpeper
1 tbsp soy sauce or browning
2 tbsp vinegar
1 stalk eskellion
½ bell pepper (assorted colors)
1-2 tsp cornstarch

Method:

1. Clean chicken. Add vinegar to bowl and chicken. Rinse and drain.
2. Add chopped basil, cilantro, thyme onion, pimento seeds, salt, b. pepper, dash of old bay seasoning; Add soy sauce and browning, put on gloves and rub in seasoning into chicken. Cover and leave to marinate for at least 30 minutes.
3. Heat oven to 375 degree. Coat chicken according to coating used. (Open shake and bake package and coat chicken according to instruction package, or crush corn flakes in food processor.) Coat and place in baking dish.
4. Turn chicken over unto the other side after 25-30 minutes and test for tenderness.
5. Make gravy if necessary by adding left-over seasonings from chicken into saucepan. Add 1-2 cups water to pot. Season to taste. Add 1 tsp corn starch to 2-4 tsp water mix and add to gravy to thicken. Stir.
6. Cover and leave to simmer for approx. 5-10 minutes.
7. Turn off flame and serve.

Serve 3-4. Enjoy

Stewed Chicken Feet

Ingredients:

1 pack chicken feet (possibly 2 lbs)
1 onion
2 cloves chopped garlic
1 pinch scotch bonnet pepper
1 uncut scotch bonnet pepper
4-6 crushed pimento seeds
1 stalk eskellion/green onion
1 sprig thyme
1 sprig cilantro
1 sprig basil
¼-1/2 tsp salt
few diced/sliced pieces bell pepper/sweet pepper of different colors
1/2- tbsp curry powder (optional). This is only used for coloring and is not used if browning and soya sauce is used
Dash of All purpose seasoning/dry seasonings
1 tbsp soya sauce
1 tbsp browning
1 pack lima bean or 1 can grace butter bean (optional)
1-2 carrots cut in small sizes

Method:

1. Clean chicken feet by rinsing in vinegar water, and chopping of nails.
2. Peel and slice onion, peel and chop eskellion, and chop basil and cilantro and add all spices to meat in a clean bowl. (Curry is optional and is only used to give meat color).
3. Rub all seasonings together and leave to marinate for approximately 30-60 minutes.
4. Heat saucepan and add chicken feet along with seasoning.
5. Add a little water to pan, swish and add to pot. Stir and cover, adjust to medium flame and allow to cook. Stirring occasionally. Do not make chicken feet stick to pot or burn. Add water in small amounts if necessary as it browns and cook.
6. Rinse lima beans if used and leave to soak with a clove of garlic. This can be cooked separately with a tbsp of butter or cooked with the chicken feet for added flavor.
7. Cook on medium flame for approximately ½ hour stirring frequently until meat is tender and loosening from the bone.
8. Peel carrots, slice and add to pot and allow carrots to cook for approx. 5 minutes.
9. Re-season the pot to taste, add uncut pepper, lower flame, canned butter bean if used. Simmer for approximately 5 minutes.

Enjoy!
Serves 6-8

Sweet & Sour Chicken

Ingredients:

2 lbs chicken
2 tbsp vinegar (white)
¼ tsp salt
½ cup olive oil
1 large onion
1 sprig thyme
2-3 stalk eskellion or green onion
½ tsp season all/old bay seasoning
pinch scotch bonnet pepper
1 clove garlic
2 tbsp lime juice
1 tbsp brown sugar
1 pinch cinnamon
2-3 tbsp tomato ketchup
1 tsp corn starch (optional)
2-4 seeds crushed pimento
1-2 tbsp soy sauce or Chinese sauce

Method

1. Clean and cut chicken in desired pieces.
2. Place chicken in pan, add vinegar and water and rinse chicken.
3. Chop or grate 1 eskellion, ½ of onion and 1 clove garlic, and add all seasonings including powder/dry seasonings.
4. Rub in all seasonings and leave to marinate for approx. 10-20 minutes.
5. Heat olive oil in saucepan/deep fat fryer. Shake off seasonings and add chicken.
6. Allow to fry until golden brown. Remove from flame and allow oil to drain.
7. In a stock pot/saucepan, add the seasonings from the chicken, ketchup, cinnamon, nutmeg, sugar, and lime juice and soya sauce..
8. Stir and lower flame allowing sauce to simmer for approx. 3-5 minutes. Mix cornstarch in a few drops of water and use to thicken if necessary.
9. Add fried chicken to sauce, stir, cover and allow to marinate on low flame for approx. 15-20 minutes stirring occasionally.
10. Reseason to taste and simmer for 2-3 more minutes
11. Stir, remove from flame and serve.

Serves 4-6
Enjoy with your favorite side dish!

Steamed Fish

Ingredients:

2 lbs whole fish
2-4 seeds pimento
1 sprig thyme
1 sprig basil (optional)
1 sprig cilantro (optional)
1/3 tsp salt
1 small onion sliced
1 tsp olive oil or a pat of butter
Dash old bay seasoning
Dash blackpeper
4-6 small okras (optional)
2 tbsp lime juice
Foil
Plate

Method:

1. Clean fish. Add lime juice in a bowl with water and fish. Drain and set aside.
2. Add salt, black pepper and old bay seasoning making sure the fish's head and inside gets seasoned.
3. Chop/slice onion, basil cilantro and add to fish, especially head and inside through opening at side. Add a few slices of onion.
4. Cover and marinate for 5-10 minutes.
5. Lay fish flat on plate, making sure all seasonings are still on fish. Place okras on or around the fish like a garnish. Add thyme, onion rings and a sprig or any remaining herbs on fish. Pour olive oil/butter on top of fish.
6. Cover fish/plate by sealing with foil; or wrap fish tightly in foil, place on baking sheet in hot oven 350 degree for 15-20 minutes and bake. Or
7. Place on top of pot of boiling water that's cooking the food provision and cook for 15-20 minutes.
8. Remove from flame or oven and serve with favorite side dish.

Serves 3 Enjoy!

White Soft Yam, Pumpkin, Green Bananas & Dumplings

Ingredients:

1 lbs dry pumpkin
1 lbs white soft yam
1 lbs flour
2-3 tbsp corn meal
1 ¼ tsp salt separated
4-6 fingers green bananas

Method:

1. Pour water in a pot approx. 2/3 full . Place on medium flame and bring to boil.
2. Add 1 tsp salt. Stir
3. Rinse pumpkin scrubbing the outer skin until clean. Remove the inside (belly), along with all seeds. Cut in 2-3 pieces and add to pot.
4. Peel yam thinly and cut in 2-3 pieces, and add to pot.
5. Rinse and peel green bananas by first cutting off the stem at the top and bottom and using the knife to open one of the seams on the side of the banana. With the side of the thumb, while holding the banana in your hand , gently peel back the skin starting at the open seam. Use a knife to scrape of any excess banana skin that might be left. Add bananas to pot. Stir
6. Place flour, cornmeal and ¼ tsp salt into a bowl..
7. Place approximately 1 cup of water nearby and an empty plate/dish.
8. Mix ingredients in bowl together and make a hole in the center.
9. Rinse hands and fingers and check finger nails for hygiene purposes.
10. Add 1/2 of the water to flour mixture and use your/hand/fingers to knead into a ball, picking up the mixture as you knead. Add remainder of water if necessary. The mixture should be of elastic consistency not tough, and bowl should be clean.
11. Pull of small pieces of mixture about the size of a regular donut. Roll in the center of your hand, while simultaneously bringing the center together. When finish, use the ball of your palm (pinkie finger side) to make a quick, light press in the center. Add each dumpling to pot and stir.
    The dumpling should look just like a donut without the hole.
12. Place plate with fish on top of pot. (Plate would serve as pot cover only for steaming fish using this method).
13. Leave food and fish to cook for 15-20 minutes or until tender. After 10-12 minutes check fish and ground provisions and remove them from pot as they cook easily and will break apart.
14. Remove from flame and serve.

Serves 3-4
Enjoy!!

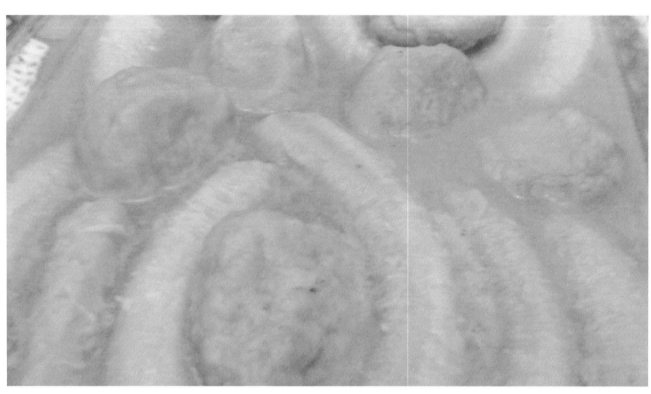

White Soft Yam, Pumpkin, Green Bananas & Dumplings

Escovitch Fish

Ingredients:

2 lbs whole fish
2-4 seeds pimento
1 sprig thyme
1 sprig basil (optional)
1 sprig cilantro (optional)
1/3 tsp salt
1 small onion sliced
1/2 cup olive oil/vegetable oil
Dash old bay seasoning
Dash black pepper
2-4 small carrots cut in thin strips
2 tbsp lime juice
1 hot pepper cut in thin strips and deseeded
2 tbsp vinegar
Foil

Method:

1. Clean fish add lime juice and water and rinse. Pat dry and lay on cutting board or plate
2. Add chopped basil, cilantro, thyme and a few slices of onion, salt, b. peeper and dash of old bay seasoning; paying special attention to head and insides sprinkling with salt, black pepper and old bay seasoning.
3. Cover and shake to distribute the seasoning. Leave to marinate 10 minutes.
4. Add ½ of oil to frying pan and heat until very hot.
5. Gently place each fish in oil and fry until crisp, turning on opposite side and frying crisp. Add remainder of oil if necessary until all fish is fried.
6. Remove and place on napkin in plate to drain off excess oil.
7. Remove excess oil from frying pan, leaving approximately 1 tbsp in frying pan. Turn off flame awhile while preparing fish.
8. Remove napkin and place fish in serving dish. Add rings of onion, strips of carrots, pepper, and pimento seeds on fish like a bed.
9. Heat sauce pan, add vinegar and seasonings remaining in bowl and sauté for 1 minute.
10. Remove from flame and pour directly on fish.
11. Seal with foil.
12. Remove foil approximately10-20 minutes after, and serve with festival or bammy.

*Fish can be headless and any type of fish can be used.

Serve 3-4
Enjoy

Escovitch Fish

Brown Stew Fish

Ingredients:
2 lbs sliced fish
2-4 seeds pimento
1 sprig thyme
1 sprig basil (optional)
1 sprig cilantro (optional)
1/3 tsp salt
1 small onion sliced
1/2 cup olive oil/vegetable oil
Dash old bay seasoning
Dash blackpeper
1 tbsp soy sauce or browning
2 tbsp lime juice
1-2 cooking tomatoes
1 stalk eskellion
½ bell pepper (assorted colors)
1 tbsp ketchup (optional)
1-2 tsp cornstarch
1tbsp white wine (optional)

Method:
1. Clean fish add lime juice and water and rinse. Pat dry and lay on cutting board or plate
2. Add chopped basil, cilantro, thyme onion, pimento seeds, salt, b. pepper, and dash of old bay seasoning; paying special attention to head and insides sprinkling with salt, black pepper and old bay seasoning. Slice tomatoes and bell peppers in small cubes and add to fish.
3. Cover and shake to distribute the seasoning. Leave to marinate 10 minutes.
4. Add ½ of oil to frying pan and heat until very hot.
5. Use a fork to gently scrape seasoning off fish. Place each fish in oil and fry until crisp, turning on opposite side and frying crisp. Add remaining oil if necessary until all fish is fried.
6. Remove and place on napkin in plate to drain off excess oil.
7. Remove excess oil from frying pan, leaving approximately 1 tbsp in frying pan.
8. Add 2 cups water to seasoning remaining in pan/bowl. Swiss around in pan and add to the heated oil on stove. Stir.
9. Add ketchup, soy sauce and browning, Stir.
10. Add dash of powder seasoning and season to taste. Add white wine and stir.
11. Add 1 tsp corn starch to 2-4 tsp water mix and add to gravy to thicken. Stir.
12. Place fried fish into gravy, lower flame, cover and leave to simmer for approx. 5-7 minutes.
13. Turn off flame and serve.

*Fish can be headless and any type of fish can be used.
Serve 3-4.
Enjoy!

Brown Stew Fish

Fried Fish

Ingredients:

2 lbs whole fish
1/3 tsp salt
1 cup olive oil/vegetable oil
Dash old bay seasoning
Dash black pepper
2 tbsp lime juice
Dash All purpose seasoning
½ lbs flour. (optional)

Method:

1. Clean fish add lime juice and water and rinse. Pat dry and lay on cutting board or plate
2. Sprinkle all seasonings on fish paying special attention to the head and inside.
3. Cover and shake to distribute the seasoning. Leave to marinate 10 minutes.
4. Add ½ of oil to frying pan and heat until very hot.
5. Place flour in a plate and add a dash of the seasonings to it.
6. Gently place each fish in flour and lightly cover. Shake off excess flour.
7. Place fish in hot oil and fry until crisp, turning on each side. Add remainder of oil if necessary until all fish is fried.
8. Remove and place on napkin in plate to drain off excess oil.
9. Serve with festival or bammy.

*Fish can be headless and any type of fish can be used.

Serve 3-4.
Enjoy!

Fried Fish

Bake Fish

Ingredients:

2-3 lbs fish (sliced or whole)
1 onion
1 cloves chopped garlic
1 pinch scotch bonnet pepper
4-6 seeds pimento
1 stalk eskellion/green onion
1 sprig thyme
1 sprig cilantro
1 sprig basil
¼-1/2 tsp salt
2-3 slices finely sliced mix bell pepper (different colors) (optional)
Dash black pepper
Dash all- purpose seasoning/dry seasonings
Dash old bay seasonings
1 tbsp lime juice

Method:

1. Clean fish, remove all scales. Add lime juice to water, rinse and drain.
2. Peel and slice onion, peel and chop eskellion, and chop basil, cilantro and add all spices to fish in a clean bowl. Add all spices and herbs, paying special attention to fish head an inside to distribute seasonings well if whole fish is used.
3. Use a disposable gloves to rub all seasonings over fish or cover with plate and shake well.
4. Leave to marinate for approximately 10-15 minutes or even overnight.
5. Heat oven to 375 degree. Place fish in casserole dish/baking pan, making sure that all seasoning is placed on the bottom of the pan like a bed of flowers and fish is placed on top. Make sure no seasoning is on top of fish. This is done so that the herbs and spices will add flavor as fish is baked, without getting burnt.
6. Cover /seal witch foil and place on 2nd rack in oven. Bake for 10 minutes remove foil.
7. Continue to bake for another 10-15 minutes basting fish with juices extracted from it while it was covered.
8. At the end of baking time fish should be tender and baked with light brown color. Fish will also make its own gravy.
9. Remove from oven and serve with your favorite side order.

PS: It should be noted that the longer fish is left to marinate the more flavorful it is.

Enjoy!
Serves 4-6

Stew Pork

Ingredients:

2 lbs fresh pork (sliced thinly or cut in 1″ length)
4-8 pimento seeds (crushed)
1 sprig thyme
1 sprig basil (optional)
1 sprig cilantro (optional)
2 cloves garlic (chopped)
1/3 tsp salt
1 small onion sliced
Dash old bay seasoning
Dash blackpeper
1 tbsp soy sauce or browning
2 tbsp vinegar
1-2 cooking tomatoes
1 stalk eskellion
½ bell pepper (assorted colors)
1-2 tsp cornstarch
1 large potato (optional)
2-3 carrots (optional)

Method:

1. Clean pork and cut as desired. Add vinegar to bowl and meat. Rinse and drain.
2. Add chopped basil, cilantro, thyme onion, pimento seeds, salt, b. pepper, dash of old bay seasoning; Slice tomatoes and bell peppers in small cubes and add to meat. Add soy sauce and browning, put on gloves and rub in seasoning into meat. Cover and leave to marinate for at least 30 minutes.
3. Heat saucepan, scrape off seasonings off meat and place in pot, cover and leave to brown and cook.
4. Turn meat over unto the other side occasionally, adding a little bit of water to prevent sticking to the bottom. Stir and cook until meat is brown and tender.
5. Add approx. 2 cups water to seasonings in bowl. Swiss. Add to pork. Stir cover.
6. Add a tsp browning soy sauce, peel, cut and dice 1-2 carrots and 1 potato. Add to pork. Stir.
7. Add dash of powder seasoning and season to taste. Add 1 tsp corn starch to 2-4 tsp water mix and add to gravy to thicken. Stir.
8. Cover and leave to simmer for approx. 5-10 minutes.
9. Turn off flame and serve.

Serve 3-4. Enjoy

Pork Chops

<u>Ingredients:</u>

2 lbs fresh pork chops
4-8 pimento seeds (crushed)
1 sprig thyme
1 sprig basil (optional)
1 sprig cilantro (optional)
2 cloves garlic (chopped)
1/3 tsp salt
1 small onion sliced
Dash old bay seasoning
Dash blackpeper
1 tbsp soy sauce or browning
2 tbsp vinegar
1 tbsp ketchup (optional)
1-2 cooking tomatoes
1 stalk eskellion
½ bell pepper (assorted colors)
1-2 tsp cornstarch
Small piece of hot pepper (skin –no seeds)

<u>Method:</u>

1. Clean chops. Add vinegar to bowl and meat. Rinse and drain.
2. Add chopped basil, cilantro, thyme onion, pimento seeds, salt, b. pepper, dash of old bay seasoning; Slice tomatoes and bell peppers in small cubes and add to meat. Add soy sauce and browning, put on gloves and rub in seasoning into meat. Cover and leave to marinate for at least 30 minutes.
3. Heat saucepan, add meat along with all seasonings. Rinse out seasoning pan, and add to pot. Cover and leave to brown and cook, stirring frequently.
4. Turn meat over unto the other side, adding a little bit of water to prevent sticking to the bottom. Stir and cook until meat is brown and tender.
5. Add water if necessary as meat cooks and brown. Don't allow it to stick or burn, and it will make its own gravy
6. Add a tsp browning/soy sauce and ketchup. Stir.
7. Add dash of powder seasoning and season to taste. Thicken gravy if necessary, using cornstarch. Stir.
8. Cover and leave to simmer for approx. 5-10 minutes.
9. Turn off flame and serve.

Serve 3-4.
Enjoy

Pork Chops

Shake & Baked Pork Chops

Ingredients:

2 lbs fresh pork chops
4-8 pimento seeds (crushed)
1 sprig thyme
1 sprig basil (optional)
1 sprig cilantro (optional)
2 cloves garlic (chopped)
1/3 tsp salt
1 small onion sliced
1 pk shake & bake pork or
1-2 cups bread crumbs or corn flakes
Dash old bay seasoning
Dash blackpeper
1 tbsp soy sauce or browning
2 tbsp vinegar
1 stalk eskellion
½ bell pepper (assorted colors)
1-2 tsp cornstarch
Small piece of hot pepper (skin –no seeds)

Method:

1. Clean meat. Add vinegar to bowl and meat. Rinse and drain.
2. Add chopped basil, cilantro, thyme onion, pimento seeds, salt, b. pepper, dash of old bay seasoning; Add soy sauce and browning, put on gloves and rub in seasoning into meat. Cover and leave to marinate for at least 30 minutes.
3. Heat oven to 375°F. Scrape seasonings off pork chop and coat according to coating used. (Open shake and bake package and coat meat according to instruction package, or crush corn flakes in food processor).
4. Beat or whish an egg. Dip chops in egg and coat with corn flakes. Place in baking dish and bake.
5. Turn meat over unto the other side after 25-30 minutes and test for tenderness, and bake for color, (that is golden brown).
6. Make gravy if necessary by adding left-over seasonings from pork chops into saucepan. Add 1-2 cups water to pot. Season to taste. Add 1 tsp corn starch to 2-4 tsp water mix and add to gravy to thicken. Stir.
7. Cover and leave to simmer for approx. 5-10 minutes.
8. Turn off flame and serve.

Serve 3-4. Enjoy

Barbeque Spare Ribs

<u>Ingredients:</u>

1 pack baby back spare ribs
1 onion
1 clove chopped garlic
1 pinch scotch bonnet pepper
4-6 seeds pimento
1 stalk eskellion/green onion
1 sprig thyme
1 sprig cilantro
1 sprig basil
¼-1/2 tsp salt
Dash of powder seasonings
2 tbsp lime juice
Pinch cinnamon
2 tbsp honey
2 tbsp vinegar
2 tbsp sugar
1 bottle Kraft Honey Smoked Barbeque Sauce
2-4 tbsp ketchup
1 tsp cornstarch

<u>Method:</u>

1. Clean meat remove excess fat and rinse in vinegar water.
2   Peel and slice onion, peel and chop eskellion, and chop basil and cilantro.
3   Add all seasonings to meat in a clean bowl. Use disposable gloves to rub all seasonings together and leave to marinate for approximately 30-60 minutes.
4   Place 1-2 cups of water in a large saucepan, enough just to cover meat.
5   Add ribs along with seasonings. Cover and boil for approximately 10 minutes. Turn off flame drain stock and put aside.
6   Heat oven to 375°F, remove meat from pot, and place in baking dish or grill.
7   Pour stock in a small bowl or pot. Add lime juice, cinnamon, honey, vinegar, sugar, ½ bottle Kraft honey hickory Smoked barbeque sauce and tomato ketchup. Stir. Mix cornstarch with a few tbsp cold water, stir and add to sauce/mixture to thicken if necessary.
8   Base ribs and place in oven/grill. Bake for 25-30 minutes until tender. Turn from side to side coating and allow to bake.
9   Turn ribs unto other side base, and allow heat to penetrate for another 5-10 minutes.

Serve 3-4. Enjoy

Barbeque Pork Chops

Ingredients:

2-3 lbs fresh pork chops
1 onion
1 clove chopped garlic
1 pinch scotch bonnet pepper
4-6 seeds pimento
1 stalk eskellion/green onion
1 sprig thyme
1 sprig cilantro
1 sprig basil
¼-1/2 tsp salt
black pepper
Dash of powder seasonings
2 tbsp lime juice
Pinch cinnamon
2 tbsp vinegar
2 tbsp honey
2 tbsp sugar
1 bottle Kraft Honey Smoked Barbeque Sauce
2-4 tbsp ketchup
1 tsp cornstarch

Method:

1. Clean meat, in vinegar water rinse and drain.
2. Peel and slice onion, peel and chop eskellion, and chop basil and cilantro.
3. Add all seasonings to meat in a clean bowl. Use a disposable gloves to rub all seasonings together and leave to marinate for approximately 30-60 minutes.
4. Heat oven to 375°F, or prepare grill. Place chops in casserole dish/baking pan.
5. Use a fork to remove herbal seasonings off the top of meat as this burn first. Place the herbs on the base of the baking dish as a bed and place chops on top of herbs.
6. Cover with foil for the 1st 15 minutes of baking and place on 2nd rack in oven.
7. Remove foil and allow chops to bake until tender. Base chops with barbeque sauce.
8. While meat is in oven, mix lime juice, cinnamon, honey, vinegar, sugar, ½ bottle Kraft honey hickory Smoked barbeque sauce and tomato ketchup. Stir. Mix cornstarch with 2-4 tbsp water and add to sauce to thicken if necessary.
9. Base pork chops and place in oven. Bake for 25-30 minutes until tender. Turn from side to side coating. Allow to bake until tender.
10. Turn chops unto other side base, and allow heat to penetrate for another 5-10 minutes.

Serve 3-4. Enjoy

Jerk Pork

<u>Ingredients:</u>

2-3 lbs fresh pork
1 onion
1 clove chopped garlic
1 pinch scotch bonnet pepper
4-6 seeds pimento
1 stalk eskellion/green onion
1 sprig thyme
1 sprig cilantro
1 sprig basil
1 tbsp browning
¼-1/2 tsp salt
2-3 tbsp Hot Grace Jerk Seasoning (Mild flavor can be used but would require more seasoning).
6-8 sliced pieces bell pepper/sweet pepper of different colors (optional)

<u>Method:</u>

1. Clean pork removing excess fat, rinse in vinegar water and cut in small pieces.
2. Peel and slice onion, peel and chop eskellion, and chop basil and cilantro.
3. Place seasonings in food processor and chop finely.
4. Remove and add all seasonings/spices along with Jerk seasoning to pork in a clean bowl. Use disposable gloves to rub all seasonings together and leave to marinate for approximately 30-60 minutes.
5. Heat oven to 375°. Place pork in casserole dish/baking pan, or pot (if done on stove top) cover with foil for the 1st 15 minutes of baking and place on 2nd rack in oven.
6. Remove foil and allow pork to bake until brown and tender. Base pork with juices extracted from meat during cooking and turning pork from side to side frequently.
7. Garnish with bell pepper slices or parsley and serve with your favorite side order.

PS

Pork can be done on a barbecue grill or stove top.

Enjoy!
Serves 4-6

Pig Trotters (Pig Feet)

<u>Ingredients:</u>

2-3 lbs pigstail
1 onion
2 cloves chopped garlic
1 pinch scotch bonnet pepper
1 uncut scotch bonnet pepper
4-6 crushed pimento seeds
1 stalk eskellion/green onion
1 sprig thyme
1 sprig cilantro
1 sprig basil
¼-1/2 tsp salt
few diced/sliced pieces bell pepper/sweet pepper of assorted colors
1/2- tbsp curry powder (optional) **This is only used for coloring and is not used if browning and soya sauce is used**
Dash of All purpose seasoning/dry seasonings
1 tbsp soya sauce
1 tbsp browning
1 pack lima bean or 1 can grace butter bean (optional)

<u>Method:</u>

1. Clean meat by rinsing in vinegar water and cut in desired sizs.
2. Peel and slice onion, peel and chop eskellion, and chop basil and cilantro and add all spices to pig trotters in a clean bowl. (Curry is optional and is only used to give meat color).
3. Rub all seasonings together and leave to marinate for approximately 30-60 minutes.
4. Rinse lima beans if used and leave to soak with a clove of garlic. This can be cooked separately with a tbsp of butter or cooked with the meat for added flavor.
5. Heat saucepan, add all seasonings. Stir and cover. Add 2-3 cups water enough to cover meat, stir.
6. Cook on medium flame for approximately 1 hour stirring frequently until meat is tender and loosening from the bone. Or, transfer contents to a pressure cooker and pressure for approximately 20-25 minutes or until tender and meat is tender.
7. Re-season the pot to taste, add uncut pepper, lower flame, canned butter bean if used. Simmer for approximately 10 minutes.

PS: It should be noted that the longer meat is left to marinate the more flavorful it is

Enjoy!
Serves 6-8

Tripe & Beans

Ingredients:

2-3 lbs tripe
1 onion
2 cloves chopped garlic
1 pinch scotch bonnet pepper
1 uncut scotch bonnet pepper
4-6 crushed pimento seeds
1 stalk eskellion/green onion
1 sprig thyme
1 sprig cilantro
1 sprig basil
¼-1/2 tsp salt
few diced/sliced pieces bell pepper/sweet pepper of different colors
1/2- tbsp curry powder (optional) .This is only used for coloring and is not used if browning and soya sauce is used
Dash of All purpose seasoning/dry seasonings
1 tbsp soya sauce
1 tbsp browning
1 pack lima bean or 1 can grace butter bean

Method:

1. Clean meat by rinsing in vinegar water, and cut in 3/8-1" size.
2. Peel and slice onion, peel and chop eskellion, and chop basil and cilantro and add all spices to meat in a clean bowl. (Curry is optional and is only used to give meat color).
3. Rub all seasonings together and leave to marinate for approximately 30-60 minutes.
4. Rinse lima beans if used and leave to soak with a clove of garlic. This can be cooked separately with a tbsp of butter or cooked with the meat for added flavor.
5. Heat saucepan, add all seasonings. Stir and cover. Ad 2-3 cups water enough to cover meat, stir.
6. Cook on medium flame for approximately 1 hour stirring frequently until meat is tender. Or, transfer contents to a pressure cooker and pressure for approximately 15-20 minutes or until tender.
7. Re-season the pot to taste, add uncut pepper, and canned butter bean if used.

8. Lower flame and simmer for approximately 10 minutes.

9. Serve.

Enjoy!
Serves 6-8

PS: It should be noted that the longer meat is left to marinate the more flavorful it is

Stew Beef

Ingredients:

2 lbs fresh beef
2 tbsp vinegar (white)
¼ tsp salt
1 small onion
1 sprig thyme
1 sprig cilantro
1 sprig basil
1 stalk eskellion or green onion
½ tsp season all/old bay seasoning
pinch scotch bonnet pepper
1 clove garlic
dash black pepper
2-4 seeds crushed pimento
1 tbsp soy sauce or Chinese sauce
1 tbsp browning
1/2 bell pepper (assorted colors optional)
2 small carrots
1 irish potato
1 tbsp olive oil

Method:

1. Clean and cut beef into small cube sizes.
2. Place meat in pan, add vinegar and water and rinse.
3. Chop or grate eskellion, onion and garlic and add all seasonings including powder/dry seasonings.
4. Rub in all seasonings and leave to marinate for approx. 10-20 minutes.
5. Heat saucepan, add olive oil. Use a fork to remove seasonings from meat
6. Add meat, stir and cover allowing meat to brown. If necessary, add a little water at a time as meat brown and cook. Do not let it burn or stick to pot.
7. Lower flame and stir occasionally.
8. When meat is fully brown add 2 cups of water to seasonings, swiss and add to meat. Cover and stir allowing meat to cook until tender; or add contents of pot to a pressure cocker and cook for approx. 10-15 minutes until tender.
9. Approximately 5 minutes before meat is fully cooked, peel and dice potatoes and carrots, and add to meat.
10. Meat will make its own gravy. Add a tbsp ketchup if desired.
11. Reseason with onion and a dash of spices if necessary.
12. Stir, remove from flame. Serve with your favorite side order.

Serve 4-6, Enjoy with your favorite side dish!

Peppered Steak

<u>Ingredients:</u>

2 lbs fresh beef or sirloin steak
2 tbsp vinegar (white)
¼ tsp salt
1 small onion
1 sprig thyme
1 sprig cilantro
1 sprig basil
1 stalk eskellion or green onion
½ tsp season all/old bay seasoning
pinch scotch bonnet pepper
1 clove garlic
dash black pepper
2-4 seeds crushed pimento
1 tbsp soy sauce or Chinese sauce
1 tbsp browning
1/2 bell pepper (assorted colors)
1 tbsp olive oil

<u>Method:</u>

1. Clean and cut beef into small cube sizes, or edible slices if sirloin is used.
2. Place meat in pan, add vinegar and water and rinse.
3. Slice bell peppers, onions, eskellion and add along with all seasonings including powder/dry seasonings.
4. Rub in all seasonings and leave to marinate for approx. 10-20 minutes.
5. Heat saucepan, add olive oil. Do not remove seasonings. Add meat along with seasonings. Swiss a little water in the bowl and add to pot.
6. Stir, cover and lower flame allowing meat to brown and cook simultaneously. If necessary, add a little water at a time as meat brown and cook. Do not let the meat or seasoning burn or stick to the pot. Cook until brown and tender.
7. Meat will make its own gravy. Add a tbsp ketchup if desired.
8. Reseason with onion, bell peppers and a dash of spices if necessary.
9. Stir, remove from flame. Serve with your favorite side order.

Serve 4-6
Enjoy with your favorite side dish!

Cow Foot and Beans

Ingredients:

2-3 lbs cow foot
1 onion
2 cloves chopped garlic
1 pinch scotch bonnet pepper
1 uncut scotch bonnet pepper
4-6 seeds pimento
1 stalk eskellion/green onion
1 sprig thyme
1 sprig cilantro
1 sprig basil
¼-1/2 tsp salt
few diced/sliced pieces bell pepper/sweet pepper of different colors
All purpose seasoning/dry seasonings
1 tbsp soya sauce
1 tbsp browning
1 pack lima bean or 1 can grace butter bean

Method:

1. Clean meat removing any fat, rinse meat in vinegar water. Cut in 1 inch sizes. This could be cut at the meat shop.
2. Peel and slice onion, peel and chop eskellion, and chop basil and cilantro and add all spices to cowfoot in a clean bowl. Use a disposable gloves to rub all seasonings together and leave to marinate for approximately 30-60 minutes or even overnight.
3. Pour contents of bowl along with seasoning in a pot with tight fitting cover or preferably a pressure cooker.
4. Rinse lima beans if used and leave to soak with a clove of garlic. This can be cooked separately and added to the cow foot or better still cooked with the meat for added flavor.
5. Add 2 ½-3 cups water stir and leave to cook until tender. If pressure cooker is used, cook for approximately 30 minutes or until tender.
6. Re-season the pot to taste, add uncut pepper, lower flame, canned butter bean if used. Simmer for approximately 10 minutes.

PS: It should be noted that the longer meat is left to marinate the more flavorful it is

Enjoy!
Serves 6-8

Cow Skin And Beans

Ingredients:

2-3 lbs cow skin
1 onion
2 cloves chopped garlic
1 pinch scotch bonnet pepper
1 uncut scotch bonnet pepper
4-6 seeds pimento
1 stalk eskellion/green onion
1 sprig thyme
1 sprig cilantro
1 sprig basil
¼-1/2 tsp salt
few diced/sliced pieces bell pepper/sweet pepper of different colors
All purpose seasoning/dry seasonings
1 tbsp soya sauce
1 tbsp browning
1 pack lima bean or 1 can grace butter bean

Method:

1. Clean meat removing any fat, rinse meat in vinegar water. Cut in 1 inch sizes.
2. Peel and slice onion, peel and chop eskellion, and chop basil and cilantro and add all spices to cowskin in a clean bowl. Use a disposable gloves to rub all seasonings together and leave to marinate for approximately 30-60 minutes or even overnight.
3. Pour contents of bowl along with seasoning in a pot with tight fitting cover or preferably a pressure cooker.
4. Rinse lima beans if used and leave to soak with a clove of garlic. This can be cooked separately and added to the cow skin or better still cooked with the meat for added flavor
5. Add 2 ½-3 cups water stir and leave to cook until tender. If pressure cooker is used, cook for approximately 30 minutes or until tender.
6. Re-season the pot to taste, add uncut pepper, lower flame, canned butter bean if used.

7. Simmer for approximately 10 minutes.

Enjoy!
Serves 6-8

Pot Roast Beef

Ingredients:

2-5 lbs fresh beef
2 tbsp vinegar (white)
¼ tsp salt
1 small onion
1 sprig thyme
1 sprig cilantro
1 sprig basil
1 stalk eskellion or green onion
½ tsp season all/old bay seasoning
pinch scotch bonnet pepper
1 clove garlic
dash black pepper
6-10 seeds crushed pimento

Method:

1. Clean meat by cutting and removing any excess fat.
2. Place meat in pan, add vinegar and water and rinse.
3. Prepare all seasonings, except powdered seasoning and mince in a food processor.
4. Remove, place in a dish and add powdered seasonings. Stir to blend together.
5. Pat dry meat, and place on a cutting board
6. Use a knife to skewer hole in the meat and use a glove to stuff seasonings into each hole in ½ tsps measurements.
7. Turn meat over from side to side skewering holes and stuffing seasoning until holes are all over the meat approximately ½ inch apart.
8. Marinate for approximately 30 minutes.
9. Heat a deep saucepan. Do not add any oil. Place meat in pan, rinse out bowl with a little water to get any remaining seasoning, swiss, and add to pot.
10. Cover tightly, lower flame and allow meat to brown and cook, stirring frequently turning meat on all sides approximately every 15 minutes.
11. Do not allow meat to burn, add a little water when stirring if meat sticks to pot.
12. Cook for approximately one hour until tender and fully brown. Test with fork for tenderness.
13. Remove from flame, place in a platter, garnish with parsley.
14. Meat should make enough gravy, but if insufficient after removing meat, add 1 cup water a little browning, mix 1 tsp corn starch and a tbsp white wine.
15. Stir, and add a dash of powder seasoning if necessary, and 1 tbsp tomato ketchup.
13. Stir, Leave to simmer for five minutes. Slice beef into thin slice and serve with gravy and favorite side order.

Serve 4-8
Enjoy with your favorite side dish!

Baked Jacketed Potatoes

<u>Ingredients:</u>

4-6 large baking potatoes or sweet potatoes

<u>Method</u>

1. Scrub and dry potatoes.
2. Use a knife to stick each potato all over to allow for easy cooking.
3. Wrap each potato in sarong wrap.
4. Place in microwave and bake giving each potato 6-8 minutes each or
5. Heat oven to 400°F, wrap each potato in aluminum foil and bake for approximately 90 minutes or until tender.

Serves 4-6
Enjoy with your roast beef

Corned Beef & Cabbage

Ingredients:

1 tin corned beef (preferably Grace)
1 tbsp vinegar (white)
2 lbs cabbage
1 small onion
1 sprig thyme
1 sprig cilantro
1 sprig basil
1 stalk eskellion or green onion
½ tsp season all/old bay seasoning
pinch scotch bonnet pepper
1 clove garlic
dash black pepper
2-4 seeds crushed pimento
1 tbsp soy sauce or Chinese sauce
1-2 cooking tomatoes
1/3 cup olive oil/vegetable oil
½ bell pepper (assorted –optional)

Method

1. Clean cabbage by removing wilted leaves. Cut in two halves.
2. Place cabbage in bowl, add vinegar and water and rinse.
3. Place on cutting board to drip off excess water. Then cut in small slices approx. 1 cm thick.
4. Cut and or chop seasonings including tomatoes and add along with pimento and powdered seasonings to cabbage. Do not mince seasonings.
5. Put on gloves and rub in seasoning or cover bowl and shake to distribute seasonings.
6. Cover and leave to marinate 5-10 minutes.
7. Heat saucepan add oil and heat. Put cabbage in oil with all its seasonings. Stir. Do not cover. This will prevent cabbage from being soggy.
8. Lower flame, and leave cabbage to cook for approximately 10 minutes, stirring frequently.
9. Open cornbeef and add to cabbage. Stir to break up the cornbeef and distribute evenly with the cabbage.
10. Cover pot and allow to simmer for approximately 3-5 minutes to make to make its own gravy.
11. Stir, remove from flame. Serve with your favorite side order.

Serve 4-6

Salt Fish & Cabbage

Ingredients:

½-1 lbs salt fish
1 tbsp vinegar (white)
2 lbs cabbage
1 small onion
1 sprig thyme
1 sprig cilantro
1 sprig basil
1 stalk eskellion or green onion
½ tsp season all/old bay seasoning
pinch scotch bonnet pepper
1 clove garlic
dash black pepper
2-4 seeds crushed pimento
1 tbsp soy sauce or Chinese sauce
1-2 cooking tomatoes
1/3 cup olive oil/vegetable oil
½ bell pepper (assorted –optional)

Method

1. Place saltfish in a bowl of cold water, refrigerate overnight if possible to remove excess salt.
2. Pour off water place in a small pot and cook for approximately 5-10 minutes or until tender.
3. Pour off water and place into a bowl of cold water.
4. Clean cabbage by removing wilted leaves. Cut in two halves.
5. Place cabbage in bowl, add vinegar and water and rinse.
6. Place on cutting board to drip off excess water. Then cut in small slices approx. 1 cm thick.
7. Cut and or chop seasonings including tomatoes and add along with pimento and powdered seasonings to cabbage. Do not mince seasonings.
8. Pour water off saltfish. Rinse your hands or put on a glove and break the fish in small pieces approximately 1 inch size. Add to the cabbage.
9. Use a gloved hand to rub in seasoning or cover bowl and shake to distribute seasonings.
10. Cover and leave to marinate 5-10 minutes.
11. Heat saucepan add oil and heat. Put cabbage in oil with all its seasonings. Stir. Do not cover. This will prevent cabbage from being soggy.
12. Lower flame, and leave cabbage to cook for approximately 10 minutes, stirring frequently.
13. Cover pot and allow to simmer for approximately 3-5 minutes to make to make its own gravy.
14. Add a dash of onion, soy sauce, bell pepper and or powdered seasonings for flavor.
15. Stir, remove from flame. Serve with your favorite side order.

Serve 4-6

Cabbage & (Mince) Ground Beef

<u>Ingredients:</u>

1-1/2 lbs ground beef
1 tbsp vinegar (white)
2 lbs cabbage
¼ tsp salt
1 small onion
1 sprig thyme
1 sprig cilantro
1 sprig basil
1 stalk eskellion or green onion
½ tsp season all/old bay seasoning
pinch scotch bonnet pepper
1 clove garlic
dash black pepper
2-4 seeds crushed pimento
1 tbsp soy sauce or Chinese sauce
1-2 cooking tomatoes
½ bell pepper (assorted –optional)

<u>Method</u>

1. Clean ground beef by rinsing in a bowl with vinegar and water.
2. Cut and or chop seasonings including tomatoes and add along with pimento and powdered seasonings to ground beef. Do not mince seasonings.
3. Put on gloves and rub in seasoning. Marinate for 10-20 minutes.
4. Heat saucepan. Do not use any oil as ground beef has its own built in fat.
5. Add ground beef with all its seasonings to pot. Stir, cover and leave to cook for approximately 20 minutes. Stirring frequently.
6. Clean cabbage by removing wilted leaves. Cut in two halves.
7. Place cabbage in bowl, add vinegar and water and rinse.
8. Place on cutting board to drip off excess water. Then cut in small slices approx. 1 cm thick.
9. Add cabbage to ground beef. Stir, cover and leave to cook for another 5 minutes, lowering flame.
10. Stir, season to taste if necessary. Add a dash of onion and bell pepper. And soy sauce for flavor.
11. Cover pot and allow to simmer for approximately 3-5 minutes to make to make its own gravy.
12. Stir, remove from flame. Serve with your favorite side order.

Serve 4-6

Meat Balls

<u>Ingredients:</u>

1-1/2 lbs ground beef
1 tbsp vinegar (white)
¼ cup vegetable oil
¼ tsp salt
1 small onion
1 sprig thyme
1 sprig cilantro
1 stalk eskellion or green onion
½ tsp season all/old bay seasoning
pinch scotch bonnet pepper
1 clove garlic
dash black pepper
2-4 seeds crushed pimento
1 tbsp soy sauce or Chinese sauce
1-2 eggs beaten (whisked)
½ lbs seasoned flour
1 tbsp ketchup

<u>Method</u>

1. Clean ground beef by rinsing in a bowl with vinegar and water.
2. Chop seasonings finely and add along with pimento and powdered seasonings to ground beef.
3. Add soya sauce and powdered seasonings
4. Put on gloves and rub in seasoning. Scoop meat in palms and roll into balls. Cover and lay aside to marinate for 10-20 minutes.
5. Heat saucepan. Add vegetable oil and heat.
6. Place eggs in a bowl and whisk. Place flour in a bowl and season with a dash of powdered seasonings.
7. Dip meat balls into egg. Remove and coat in seasoned flour. Shake off excess flour and place in hot oil.
8. Fry meat balls quickly until brown. Remove and place in bowl that meat was seasoned in.
9. Remove excess oil from saucepan after frying, leaving approximately 1 tbsp oil in the saucepan. Add fresh slices of onion and bell peppers to meat balls, add to saucepan.
10. Add 2 cups water add 1 tbsp ketchup and reseason with a dash of powdered seasonings.
11. Stir, cover, lower flame and allow meat malls to cook until tender for approximately 10 minutes. Meat balls will make its own gravy while simmering.
12. Stir, remove from flame. Serve with your favorite side order.

Serve 4-6

Corned Beef & Spaghetti/Macaroni)

Ingredients:

1 tin corned beef (preferably Grace)
1 tbsp vinegar (white)
1/2 pk spaghetti or macaroni
1 onion
1 sprig thyme
1 sprig cilantro
1 sprig basil
1 stalk eskellion or green onion
½ tsp season all/old bay seasoning
pinch scotch bonnet pepper
1 clove garlic
dash black pepper
2-4 seeds crushed pimento
1 tbsp soy sauce or Chinese sauce
1-2 cooking tomatoes
1/3-1/4 cup olive oil/vegetable oil
½ bell pepper (assorted –optional)

Method

1. Place a small pot on flame and bring to boil.
2. Add spaghetti or macaroni. Stir, remove cover, lower flame and allow to cook until tender.
3. Remove from flame, pour into a colander. Rinse with cold water and drain.
4. Cut and or chop seasonings including tomatoes. Do not mince seasonings.
5. Heat saucepan add oil and heat. Add chopped seasonings to heated oil. Be careful not to splash to prevent accident.
6. Stir, and lower flame. Add drained spaghetti to seasonings. Stir.
7. Open cornbeef and add to spaghetti. Stir to break up the cornbeef and distribute evenly with the spaghetti.
8. Cover pot and allow to simmer for approximately 3-5 minutes to make to make its own gravy.
9. Add a dash of powdered seasonings to flavor and pimentos.
10. Add soy sauce for flavor and coloring
11. Stir, remove from flame. Serve with your favorite side order.

Serve 4-6

Corned Beef & Rice

Ingredients:

1 tin corned beef (preferably Grace)
1 tbsp vinegar (white)
1 small onion
1 sprig thyme
1 sprig cilantro
1 sprig basil
1 stalk eskellion or green onion
½ tsp season all/old bay seasoning
pinch scotch bonnet pepper
1 clove garlic
dash black pepper
2-4 seeds crushed pimento
1-2 small cooking tomatoes
1/3 cup olive oil/vegetable oil
½ bell pepper (assorted –optional)

Method

1. Cut and or chop seasonings including tomatoes. Do not mince seasonings. Set aside.
2. Open corned beef, remove from container and set aside.
3. Heat saucepan, add oil and heat.
4 Add corned beef and stir.
5. Add remaining seasonings, stir and cover.
6. Lower flame, Stir, leave to simmer for 3-5 minutes.
7. Remove from flame and serve with rice or your favorite side dish.

Serves 4-6
Enjoy !

Macaroni & Saltfish Stew

Ingredients:

1 lbs salt fish
1 lbs pack macaroni or spaghetti
1 small onion
1 sprig thyme
1 sprig cilantro
1 sprig basil
1 stalk eskellion or green onion
½ tsp season all/old bay seasoning
pinch scotch bonnet pepper
1 clove garlic
dash black pepper
2-4 seeds crushed pimento
1 tbsp soy sauce or Chinese sauce
1-2 cooking tomatoes
1/3-1/4 cup olive oil/vegetable oil
½ bell pepper (assorted –optional)

Method

1. Place saltfish in a bowl with cold water to soak preferably overnight.
2. Drain water. Place in a pot with fresh water and boil for approximately 10 minutes or until tender.
3. Drain, place in a bowl with fresh water and place aside. (This process allows for desalting of the fish.)
4. Bring pot to boil and place macaroni to cook until tender. Do not cover while boiling. Stir. Drain in a colander, with cold water and lay aside.
5. Drain water from salt fish and break up fish in edible sizes (1 inch).
7. Cut and or chop seasonings including tomatoes and add to salt fish.
8. Heat saucepan add oil and heat. Add seasonings and salt fish. Stir. Add macaroni and stir. Add pimento and powdered seasonings. Add soy sauce. Stir.
9. Cover. Lower flame and allow to simmer for 5-7 minutes.
10. Stir, remove from flame. Serve with your favorite side order.

Serve 4-6

Okra & Saltfish Stew

Ingredients:

½ lbs salt fish
1 dozen okras
1 small onion
1 sprig thyme
1 sprig cilantro
1 sprig basil
1 stalk eskellion or green onion
½ tsp season all/old bay seasoning
pinch scotch bonnet pepper
1 clove garlic
dash black pepper
2-4 seeds crushed pimento
1-2 cooking tomatoes
1/3 cup olive oil/vegetable oil
½ bell pepper (assorted –optional)

Method

1. Place saltfish in a bowl with cold water to soak preferably overnight.
2. Drain water. Place in a pot with fresh water and boil for approximately 10 minutes or until tender.
3. Drain, place in a bowl with fresh water and place aside. (This process allows for desalting of the fish.)
4. Bring pot to boil and place okra to cook until tender. Do not cover while boiling. Stir. Drain in a colander, and lay aside.
5. Drain water from salt fish and break up fish in edible sizes (1 inch).
6. Cut and or chop seasonings including tomatoes and add to salt fish.
8. Heat saucepan add oil and heat. Add seasonings and salt fish. Stir. Add okra stir.
9. Add pimento and powdered seasonings. Add soy sauce. Stir.
10. Cover. Lower flame and allow to simmer for 5-7 minutes.
11. Stir, remove from flame. Serve with your favorite side order.

Serve 4-6
Enjoy!

Okra & Saltfish Stew

Saltfish Stew

<u>Ingredients:</u>

¾-1 lb salt fish
1 medium sized onion
1 sprig thyme
1 sprig cilantro
1 sprig basil
1 stalk eskellion or green onion
½ tsp season all/old bay seasoning
pinch scotch bonnet pepper
1 clove garlic
dash black pepper
2-4 seeds crushed pimento
2-4 cooking tomatoes
1/4 cup olive oil/vegetable oil
½ bell pepper (assorted –optional)

<u>Method</u>

1. Place saltfish in a bowl with cold water to soak preferably overnight.
2. Drain water. Place in a pot with fresh water and boil for approximately 10 minutes or until tender.
3. Drain, place in a bowl with fresh water and place aside. (This process allows for desalting of the fish.)
4. Drain water from salt fish and break up fish in edible sizes (1 inch).
5. Cut and or chop seasonings including tomatoes and add to salt fish.
6. Heat saucepan add oil and heat. Add seasonings and salt fish. Stir.
7. Add pimento and powdered seasonings. Add soy sauce. Stir.
8. Cover. Lower flame and simmer for approximately 5 minutes.
9. Stir, remove from flame. Serve with your favorite side order such as dumpling, yam and green bananas.

Serve 4-6
Enjoy!

Saltfish Stew

Butter Bean & Saltfish

Ingredients:

½ lbs salt fish
2 cans grace butter beans
1 small onion
1 sprig thyme
1 sprig cilantro
1 stalk eskellion or green onion
½ tsp season all/old bay seasoning
pinch scotch bonnet pepper
1 clove garlic
dash black pepper
2-4 seeds crushed pimento
1-2 cooking tomatoes
1/3 cup olive oil/vegetable oil
½ bell pepper (green –optional)

Method

1. Place saltfish in a bowl with cold water to soak preferably overnight.
2. Drain water. Place in a pot with fresh water and boil for approximately 10 minutes or until tender.
3. Drain, place in a bowl with fresh water and place aside. (This process allows for desalting of the fish.)
4. Drain water from salt fish and break up fish in edible sizes (1 inch).
5. Cut and or chop seasonings including tomatoes and add to salt fish.
6. Rinse the top of cans of butter beans, open and place aside. Do not drain.
7. Heat saucepan add oil and heat. Add seasonings and salt fish. Stir. Add butter beans. Stir. Add pimento and powdered seasonings. Stir.
8. Cover. Lower flame and allow to simmer for 5-7 minutes.
9. Stir, remove from flame. Serve with your favorite side order.

Serve 4-6
Enjoy!

ACKEE AND SALTFISH JAMAICA'S NATIONAL DISH

Ackee & Saltfish

<u>Ingredients:</u>

1 lbs salt fish
1 ½ dozen ackees or 2 cans ackee in brine
1 onion
1 sprig thyme
1 sprig cilantro
1 sprig basil
1 stalk eskellion or green onion
½ tsp season all/old bay seasoning
pinch scotch bonnet pepper
1 clove garlic
dash black pepper
2-4 seeds crushed pimento
1-2 cooking tomatoes
1/3-1/4 cup olive oil/vegetable oil
½ bell pepper (assorted –optional)

<u>Method</u>

1. Place saltfish in a bowl with cold water to soak preferably overnight.
2. Drain water. Bring pot to boil. Clean and rinse ackee with cold water and place in boiling water along with salt fish to cook for approximately 10 minutes or until tender.
3. Remove fish, place in bowl of cold water. Drain ackees in colander and put aside.
4. Drain water from salt fish and break up fish in edible sizes (1inch).
5. Cut and or chop seasonings including tomatoes, onions and bell peppers.
6. Heat saucepan add oil and heat. Add seasonings and salt fish. Stir. Add ackees, stir. Add pimento and powdered seasonings.
7. Cover. Lower flame and allow to simmer for 5-7 minutes.
8. Stir, remove from flame. Serve with your favorite side order.

Serve 4-6
Enjoy!

Ackee & Saltfish

Ackee & Red Herring

Ingredients:

1 medium sized red herring
1 ½ dozen ackees or 2 cans ackee in brine
1 onion
1 sprig thyme
1 sprig cilantro
1 sprig basil
1 stalk eskellion or green onion
½ tsp season all/old bay seasoning
pinch scotch bonnet pepper
1 clove garlic
dash black pepper
2-4 seeds crushed pimento
1-2 cooking tomatoes
1/3-1/4 cup olive oil/vegetable oil
½ bell pepper (assorted –optional)

Method

1. Roll a piece of paper into a statch. Put a match to it. Hold the herring above the flame giving it a quick roast. Do not burn.
2. Place herring in a bowl with cold water to soak preferably overnight.
2. Drain water. Strip or peal skin from herring. Break into small edible pieces approximately 1 inch size and put aside.
3. Clean and rinse ackee with cold water. Bring pot to boil. Add ackees, cover. Allow to cook for approximately 10 minutes or until tender..
4. Drain ackees in colander and put aside.
5. Cut and or chop seasonings including tomatoes onion and bell peppers.
6. Heat saucepan add oil and heat. Add seasonings and herring. Stir. Add ackees, stir. Add pimento and powdered seasonings.
7. Cover. Lower flame and allow to simmer for 5-7 minutes.
8. Stir, remove from flame. Serve with your favorite side order.

**Roasting adds a special flavor to the herring.

Serve 4-6
Enjoy!

Red Peas Soup

Ingredients:

1 pk red peas (kidney beans)
2 lbs irish potato
small piece ginger (shredded)
1 clove garlic
4-6 seeds pimentos
1 cup coconut milk
¼ green breadfruit (preferably yellow heart)
2 lbs sweet potatoes
1 lbs cassava or coco
1 lbs yam (white, sweet or yellow)
2 stalks eskellion
1 sprig thyme
black pepper
1 hot green pepper
1 lbs flour
¼ lbs corn meal
1lbs chicken
1 sprig cilantro
½ lbs pigtail or salt beef
meat /bone from left over turkey or ham

Method:

1. Rinse peas, crush garlic and add to peas. Leave to soak in the pot soup will be cooked in, preferably overnight as soaking reduces cooking time.
2. Place pigstail or salt beef in a bowl of cold water to soak preferably overnight. This helps to reduce salt.
3. Place pigstail/salt beef in a pot of fresh water and scald/boil for approximately 15 minutes. This further reduces salt.
4. Place stock pot or soup pot with peas on flame. Cover.
5. Add coconut milk and 3-4 cups of water. Stir and bring to a boil.
6. Chop pigtail in small pieces, and place in pot.
7. Add ham bone and any bone/turkey cuttings.
8. Clean chicken by removing fat and skin. Chop in small pieces, rinse in vinegar water and add to pot.
9. Peel ground provisions, cutting potatoes if necessary, slicing yam and breadfruit. and add to pot, stir and keep covered.
10. Sieve flour, add cornmeal and a pinch of salt. Mix ingredients together. Add approx. 1 cup water in small quantities as needed. Mix and knead flour.

11. Make dumplings and add to soup. Stir.
12. Rinse and crush eskellion, thyme, crush or shred ginger and other spices and add to soup. Add pepper whole. (Do not cut; this is for flavor)
13. Stir, Lower flame and leave to cook for approx. 30 minutes or until peas and meat are tender. Check ground provisions especially yam. Remove them if they are cooked to prevent them from breaking up in the soup. These can be added back to the soup when it is fully ready.
14. Add black pepper and a dash of powdered seasonings.
15. Remove from flame and serve hot!

Enjoy

Serves 4-6

Guango Peas (Pigeon) Soup

Ingredients:

2 pk green guango peas or 2-3 large cans guango (pigeon) or
1 pack dry guango peas
2 lbs irish potato
small piece ginger
1 clove garlic
4-6 seeds pimentos
1 cup coconut milk
2 lbs sweet potatoes
¼ green breadfruit (preferably yellow heart)
1 lbs cassava or coco
1 lbs yam (white, sweet or yellow)
2 stalks eskellion
1 sprig thyme
black pepper
1 hot green pepper
1lbs flour
¼ lbs corn meal
1lbs chicken
1 sprig cilantro
½ lbs pigtail or salt beef
meat /bone from left over turkey or ham

Method:

1   Rinse peas, crush garlic and add to peas. Leave to soak in the pot soup will be cooked in, preferably overnight as soaking reduces cooking time. **(SOAK ONLY IF DRY GUANGO IS USED)**
2   Place pigstail or salt beef in a bowl of cold water to soak preferably overnight. This helps to reduce salt.
3   Place pigstail/salt beef in a pot of fresh water and scald/boil for approximately 15 minutes. This further reduces salt.
4   Place stock pot or soup pot with peas on flame. Cover.
5   Add coconut milk and 3-4 cups of water. Stir and bring to a boil.
6   Chop pigtail in small pieces, and place in pot.
7   Add ham bone and any bone/turkey cuttings.
8   Clean chicken by removing fat and skin. Chop in small pieces, rinse in vinegar water and add to pot.
9   Peel ground provisions, cutting potatoes if necessary, and slicing yam and breadfruit in 1 ½ cm thick. and add to pot, stir and keep covered.

10 Sieve flour, add cornmeal and a pinch of salt. Mix ingredients together. Add approx. 1 cup water in small quantities as needed. Mix and knead flour.

11 Make dumplings and add to soup. Stir.

12 Rinse and crush eskellion, thyme, shred ginger and other spices and add to soup. Add pepper whole. (Do not cut; this is for flavor)

13 Stir, Lower flame and leave to cook for approx. 30 minutes or until peas and meat are tender. Check ground provisions especially yam. Remove them if they are cooked to prevent them from breaking up in the soup. These can be added back to the soup when it is fully ready.

14 Add black pepper and a dash of powdered seasonings.

15 Remove from flame and serve hot!

Enjoy
Serves 4-6

Chicken Feet/Vegetable Soup

<u>Ingredients:</u>

2 pks chicken feet or 1 lbs chicken feet
2 lbs irish potato
2-3 large carrots
1 clove garlic
4-6 seeds pimentos
1 ½ lbs pumpkin
1 cho- cho (cayote)
¼ breadfruit (preferably yellow heart)
1 small turnip
1 lbs yam (white, sweet or yellow)
2 stalks eskellion
1 sprig thyme
black pepper
1 hot green pepper
1 lbs flour
¼ lbs corn meal
1 lbs chicken or chicken back
1 sprig cilantro
½ dozen okras (Optional)
1 pk Grace Cock Soup

<u>Method:</u>

1. Place approximately 3-4 cups of water in a stock/soup pot.
2. Chop nails of chicken feet. Clean chicken/back by removing skin and fat.
3. Rinse all meat in vinegar water and add to pot. Cover and bring to boil.
4. Peel pumpkin and cut in small dices add to pot and allow to cook.
5. Peel remaining vegetables, slicing carrots, cutting cho-cho in small dices along with turnip. Rinse in water and add to pot.
6. Peel ground provisions, cutting potatoes if necessary, and slicing yam and breadfruit. and add to pot, stir and keep covered.
7. Sieve flour, add cornmeal and a pinch of salt. Mix ingredients together. Add approx. 1 cup water in small quantities as needed. Mix and knead flour.
8. Make dumplings and add to soup. Stir.
9. Rinse and crush eskellion, thyme, and other spices and add to soup. Add pepper whole. (Do not cut; this is for flavor)
10. Stir, Lower flame and leave to cook for approx. 30 minutes. Pumpkin would have mashed to a pulp giving the soup color. Check ground provisions. Remove them if they are cooked to

prevent them from breaking up in the soup. These can be added back to the soup when it is fully ready.

11. Add Grace Cock Soup Noodle, Stir.
12. Simmer for another 5 minutes.
13. Add black pepper and a dash of powdered seasonings. Season to taste.
14. Remove from flame and serve hot!

Enjoy! Serves 4-6

Fish Tea Soup

Ingredients:

2 lbs fish (preferably doctor, but any salt water fish)
1 lbs irish potato
1 clove garlic
4-6 seeds pimentos
1 cho- cho (cayote)
4-6 okras
2-3 fingers green bananas
2-3 carrots
3-6 stalks chopped callooo or spinach
1 lbs yam (white, or yellow)
2 stalks eskellion
1 sprig thyme
black pepper
1 hot green pepper
1lbs flour
1 pk Grace Cock Soup Noodle
¼ lbs corn meal
1 sprig cilantro

Method:

1. Place approximately 3-4 cups of water in a stock/soup pot.
2. Clean fish and de-bone. Add a little lime juice to water and rinse fish.
3. Add to pot, cover and bring to boil.
4. Peel vegetables, slicing carrots, cutting cho-cho in small dices along with turnip, rinse in water and add to pot. Add chopped callaloo or spinach.
5. Peel ground provisions, cutting potatoes if necessary, and slicing yam. Rinse and add to pot, stir and keep covered.
6. Rinse green bananas, cut off top and bottom stems, make a slice down the seam of the banana. Do not peel. Cut each banana into 3 pieces and add to pot.
7. Remove the top and bottom stems of each okra; rinse and add to pot.
8. Sieve flour, add cornmeal and a pinch of salt. Mix ingredients together. Add approx. 1 cup water in small quantities as needed. Mix and knead flour.
9. Make "Spinners dumplings" and add to soup. Stir.
10. Rinse and crush eskellion, thyme, and add other spices to soup. Add pepper whole. (Do not cut; this is for flavor)
11. Stir, Lower flame and leave to cook for approx. 30 minutes. Check ground provisions. Remove them if they are cooked to prevent them from breaking up in the soup. These can be added back to the soup when it is fully ready.

12. Add Grace Cock Soup Noodle, Stir.
13. Simmer for another 5 minutes.
14. Add black pepper, pimento and a dash of powdered seasonings. Season to taste.
15. Remove from flame and serve hot!

Enjoy! Serves 4-6

Goat Head Soup or (Manish Water)

<u>Ingredients:</u>

2-3 lbs goat head
1 pk chicken feet
½ lbs goat tripe
2 lbs irish potato
2-3 large carrots
1 clove garlic
4-6 seeds pimentos
½ dozen okras
½ dozen green bananas
1 lbs pumpkin
1 cho- cho (cayote)
1 small turnip
1 lbs yam (white, sweet or yellow)
2 stalks eskellion
1 sprig thyme
½ lbs coco/dasheen
black pepper
1 hot green pepper
1 lbs flour
¼ lbs corn meal
1 lbs chicken or chicken back
1 sprig cilantro
1 pk Grace Cock Soup

<u>Method:</u>

1. Place approximately 3-4 cups of water in a stock/soup pot.
2. Chop nails of chicken feet. Clean chicken/back by removing skin and fat.
3. Rinse all meat in vinegar water and add to pot. Cover and bring to boil.
4. Peel pumpkin and cut in small dices add to pot and allow to cook.
5. Peel remaining vegetables, slicing carrots, cutting cho-cho in small dices along with turnip. Rinse in water and add to pot. Add chopped callaloo or spinach.
6. Peel ground provisions, cutting potatoes if necessary, and slicing yam. and add to pot, stir and keep covered.
7. Rinse green bananas, cut off top and bottom stems, make a slice down the seam of the banana. Do not peel. Cut each banana into 3 pieces and add to pot.
8. Remove the top and bottom stems of each okra, rinse and add to pot.
9. Sieve flour, add cornmeal and a pinch of salt. Mix ingredients together. Add approx. 1 cup water in small quantities as needed. Mix and knead flour.

10. Make "Spinners dumplings" and add to soup. Stir.
11. Rinse and crush eskellion, thyme, and other spices and add to soup. Add pepper whole. (Do not cut; this is for flavor)
12. Stir, Lower flame and leave to cook for approx. 30 minutes or until all meats are tender. Check ground provisions. Remove them if they are cooked to prevent them from breaking up in the soup. These can be added back to the soup when it is fully ready.
13. Add Grace Cock Soup Noodle, Stir.
14. Simmer for another 5 minutes.
15. Add black pepper and a dash of powdered seasonings.
16. Remove from flame and serve hot!

Enjoy!
Serves 4-6

Pepper-Pot Soup

Ingredients:

½ lb pigs tail
1 pk chicken feet
½ lbs goat tripe
2 lbs irish potato
2-3 large carrots
1 clove garlic
4-6 seeds pimentos
½ dozen okras
3-4 green bananas
1 lbs pumpkin
1 cho- cho (cayote)
1 small turnip
1 lbs yam (white, sweet or yellow)
2 stalks eskellion
1 sprig thyme
black pepper
1 hot green pepper
1 lbs flour
1 lbs coco
¼ lbs corn meal
1lbs chicken or chicken back
1 sprig cilantro
1 pk Grace Cock Soup
10-12 stalks callaloo or spinach
½ lbs salt beef
1 stalk of coco leaf (engine tail)

Method:

1. Place pigstail and salt beef in a bowl. Add water place in refrigerator to soak. (preferably overnight).
2. Drain water. Pour fresh water on and place in stockpot to boil or scald for approximately 10 minutes. Drain, pour fresh water on and leave to soak.
3. Place approximately 3-4 cups of water in a stock/soup pot.
4. Chop nails of chicken feet. Clean chicken/back by removing skin and fat.
5. Rinse poultry in vinegar and water and add to pot. Cut the tripe in small one inch sizes, in vinegar and water and add to pot.
6. Drain water from salt beef and vinegar. Chop in small pieces, and add to pot.
7. Strip callaloo, place in bowl, soak in vinegar and water for a minute. Drain.

8. Cut or chop callaloo into small sizes, Add to pot.
9. Strip stem of coco leaf, soak leaf in vinegar water. Drain and chop in small pieces. Add to pot. Stir and cover.
10. Peel pumpkin and cut in small dices add to pot and allow to cook.
11. Peel remaining vegetables, slicing carrots, cutting cho-cho, coco and turnip in small dices. Rinse in water and add to pot.
12. Add chopped callaloo or spinach.
13. Peel ground provisions, cutting potatoes if necessary, slicing yam. and add to pot, stir and keep covered.
14. Rinse green bananas, cut off top and bottom stems, make a slice down the seam of the banana. Do not peel. Cut each banana into 3-6 pieces. Add to pot.
15. Remove the top and bottom stems of each okra, rinse and add to pot.
16. Sieve flour, add cornmeal and a pinch of salt. Mix ingredients together. Add approx. 1 cup water in small quantities as needed. Mix and knead flour.
17. Make "Spinners dumplings" and add to soup. Stir.
18. Crush eskellion, thyme, crush ginger and other spices and add to soup. Add pepper whole. (Do not cut; this is for flavor)
19. Stir, Lower flame and leave to cook for approx. 30-45 minutes or until all meats are tender. Check ground provisions. Remove them if they are cooked to prevent them from breaking up in the soup. These can be added back to the soup when it is fully ready.
20. Add Grace Cock Soup Noodle, Stir.
21. Simmer for another 5-10 minutes. Stir
22. Add black pepper, pimento and a dash of powdered seasonings.
23. Remove from flame and serve hot!

Enjoy! Serves 4-6

Beef Soup

Ingredients:

1 lbs fresh beef with bone
2 lbs irish potato
2-3 large carrots
1 clove garlic
4-6 seeds pimentos
1 ½ lbs pumpkin
¼ breadfruit (preferably yellow heart)
1 cho- cho (cayote)
1 small turnip
1 lbs yam (white, sweet or yellow)
2 stalks eskellion
1 sprig thyme
black pepper
1 hot green pepper
1lbs flour
¼ lbs corn meal
1 sprig cilantro
½ dozen okras (Optional)
1 pk Grace Cock Soup

Method:

1. Place approximately 3-4 cups of water in a stock/soup pot.
2. Clean meat by removing excess fat and rinse in vinegar water.
3. Add to pot, cover and bring to a boil
4. Peel pumpkin and cut in small dices add to pot and allow to cook.
5. Peel remaining vegetables, slicing carrots, cutting cho-cho in small dices along with turnip. Rinse in water and add to pot.
6. Peel ground provisions, cutting potatoes if necessary, and slicing yam and breadfruit. Add to pot, stir and keep covered.
7. Sieve flour, add cornmeal and a pinch of salt. Mix ingredients together. Add approx. 1 cup water in small quantities as needed. Mix and knead flour.
8. Make dumplings and add to soup. Stir.
9. Rinse and crush eskellion, thyme, crush ginger and other spices and add to soup. Add pepper whole. (Do not cut; this is for flavor)
10. Stir, Lower flame and leave to cook for approx. 30 minutes. Pumpkin would have mashed to a pulp giving the soup color. Check ground provisions. Remove them if they are cooked to prevent them from breaking up in the soup. These can be added back to the soup when it is fully ready.

11. Add Grace Cock Soup Noodle, Stir.
12. Simmer for another 5 minutes.
13. Add black pepper and a dash of powdered seasonings. Season to taste.
14. Remove from flame and serve hot!

Enjoy! Serves 4-6

Green Guango & Saltfish Stew

Ingredients:

2 pks green guango or 2 large tin green guango
1/2 lbs salt fish
black pepper
powered seasonings
1 hot green pepper
3-6 seeds pimento
1 clove garlic
1 onion
2 stalk eskellion
small piece ginger (shredded)
sprig thyme
sprig cilantro
sprig basil
1 cup coconut milk
1-2 tomatoes
1/3-14 cup olive or vegetable oil

Method:

1. Place saltfish in a bowl with cold water to soak preferably overnight.
2. Rinse peas, add garlic with 1 cup water and bring to a boil.
3. Add coconut milk and bring to boil. Cover and allow peas to cook until tender, soaking up all the liquid. Stir, and add water if necessary.
4. Drain water from saltfish, place in a pot with fresh water .
5. Cook for approximately 10 minutes or until tender.
6. Remove from flame, drain, and place in a bowl of cold water. (This process allows for desalting of the fish).
7. Drain water from fish and break into small pieces, approximately 1 inch size. Put aside.
8. Cut up all seasonings and spices do not mince.
9. Heat saucepan. Add cooking oil and heat. Add chopped seasonings and saltfish. Stir.
10. Add guango peas. Stir the mixture together.
11. Lower flame. Add hot pepper. Do not cut.
12. Add pimento, black pepper and dash of powdered spices.
13. Stir. Allow to simmer for 5 minutes.
14. Remove serve with favorite side dish.

Enjoy!
Serves 3-4

Susumber, Ackee & Saltfish Stew

Ingredients:

2 large bunches susumber picked and cleaned
1/2 lbs salt fish
1 dozen ackees picked and cleaned or 1 can ackee in brine
black pepper
powered seasonings
1 hot green pepper
3-6 seeds pimento
1 clove garlic
1 onion
2 stalk eskellion
sprig thyme
sprig cilantro
sprig basil
1-2 tomatoes
1/3-1/4 cup olive or vegetable oil

Method:

1. Place saltfish in a bowl with cold water to soak preferably overnight.
2. Drain water from saltfish, place in a pot with fresh water and bring to boil.
3. Rinse ackees and susumber and place in pot with salt fish. Allow items to cook. Fish should cook in approximately 10 minutes.
4. Remove place in a bowl with cold water.
5. Allow susumber and ackees to cook until tender, testing with a fork. Do not allow ackees to over cook and become soggy.
6. Drain ackee and susumber in a colander. Set aside.
7. Drain water from fish and break into small pieces, approximately 1 inch size. Set aside.
8. Cut up all seasonings and spices do not mince.
9. Heat saucepan. Add cooking oil and heat. Add chopped seasonings and saltfish. Stir.
10. Add ackee and susumber. Stir the mixture together.
11. Lower flame. Add hot pepper. Do not cut.
12. Add pimento, black pepper and dash of powdered spices.
13. Stir. Allow to simmer for 5 minutes.
14. Remove serve with favorite side dish.

Enjoy!
Serves 4-6

Kidney And Green Bananas

Ingredients:

2 lbs kidney
black pepper
powered seasonings
small piece hot green pepper
3-6 seeds pimento
1 clove garlic
1 onion
2 stalk eskellion
sprig thyme
sprig cilantro
sprig basil
1-2 tomatoes
1 tbsp browning
1 tbsp soy sauce
¼ tsp salt
1/3 olive or vegetable oil
1 tbsp tomato ketchup (optional)

Method:

1. Clean meat by removing excess fat. Cut in small 1 cm sizes. Place in a clean bowl and rinse with lime juice.
2. Chop or cut up seasoning/ spices. Do not mince. Add all seasonings and spices to meat inclusive of browning and soy sauce.
3. Use gloved hands to rub all seasonings together and leave to marinate for approximately 30 minutes or longer.
4. Heat saucepan. Add oil and heat. Add meat and all seasonings to pot.
5. Rinse bowl with a little water, swish and add to pot.
6. Stir and cover. Lower flame and leave to cook. Meat will cook and brown at the same time making its own gravy.
7. Cook until tender for approximately 25-30 minutes stirring frequently. Do not allow meat to burn. Add a little water if necessary.
8. Add ketchup, stir. Reseason to taste.
9. Add slices of onion on top. Stir. Simmer for another 2-3 minutes.
10. Remove from flame and serve with your favorite side dish.

Enjoy!
Serves 4-6

(Pickled) Salt Mackerel With Dumpling & Green Bananas

<u>Ingredients:</u>

1 large salted mackerel
2 cooking tomatoes
1 onion
2 stalk eskellion
½ bell pepper
4-6 pimentos
1/4 cup vegetable oil
Pinch scotch bonnet pepper
black pepper
dash powdered seasonings

<u>Method:</u>

1. Place mackerel in a bowl of cold water, preferably overnight to remove excess salt.
2. Drain water and place in a pot of cold water. Bring to boil. Allow to cook for approximately 10 minutes or until tender.
3. Remove from pot, place in a bowl of cold water and lay aside.
4. Chop or cut onion, eskellion, bell pepper, scotch bonnet pepper and tomatoes. Do not mince.
5. Drain water from mackerel and use a gloved hand to break the mackerel into edible pieces, approximately 1-1/2 inches. Do not discard the central bone or head of this fish.
6. Heat saucepan. Pour in vegetable oil and heat.
7. Add chopped seasonings. Stir. Add mackerel. Stir.
8. Lower flame. Add pimento and dry seasonings. Stir.
9. Cover and allow to simmer for approx. 5 minutes.
10. Stir, remove from flame and serve with green bananas and dumpling. (See recipe).

Serves 4-6
Enjoy!

(Pickled) Salt Mackerel With Dumpling & Green Bananas

Mackerel & Run Down

Ingredients:

1 lbs picked mackerel or 2 cans grace mackerel
1 dry coconut or 1 can coconut milk
1-2 cooking tomatoes
1 small onion
2 stalk eskellion
1 sprig thyme
1 clove garlic
4-6 seeds pimentos
Black pepper
Dash dry seasonings

Method:

1. Prepare dry coconut by husking, cutting in small pieces, approx. 1 cm sizes.
2. Clean, then place in blender with approx. 2-3 cups measured water and blend smooth and creamy; or open canned coconut milk. Fill can approx. 3 times and boil.
3   Place pickled mackerel in a bowl of cold water, preferably over night in the Refrigerator to remove the salt.
4. Cut or chop seasonings and set aside
6. Pour coconut milk in pot , lower flame and allow to boil. Do not cover.
8. Scrape the sides of the coconut off the side of the pot frequently as it boils.
9. Allow the coconut milk to boil until a custard/thick cream forms on the top with a natural oil.
10. While milk is boiling open cans of mackerel or drain water off pickled mackerel.
11. Place in pot with cold water and boil for approximately 10 minutes or until tender.
12. Drain, pour cold water on mackerel and set aside.
13. Drain mackerel and break into small edible pieces, approximately 1 inch sizes.
14. Add seasonings to the pot with coconut milk. Stir.
15. Add mackerel, Stir.
16. Add powdered seasonings. Cover and leave to simmer for approx. 3-7 minutes.
17. Remove from flame. Stir. Serve with your favorite side orders.

*Mackerel can be substituted for saltfish

Serves 4-6
Enjoy!

Festival

Ingredients:

3/4 lbs sifted cornmeal
¼ lbs sifted flour
½ tsp baking powder
½ tsp salt
2-3 tbsp sugar
1 cup vegetable oil
1/3 cup milk
½ -1 cup ice cold water

Method:

1. Place the flour, sugar a baking powder and salt in a bowl.
2. Make a hole in the center of the mixture.
3. Add the milk and water knead into a dough. Continue kneading using the
   tips of the finger to knead until all the mixture is taken up, leaving the bowl clean.
4. Heat saucepan. Add vegetable oil and heat.
5. Break of small pieces of dough, ball size. Knead into a dumpling/ball shape, then shape flat by
   using the finger tips to flatten from the center outwards.
6. Place in hot oil, lower flame and fry until golden brown.
7. Place in bowl lined with a paper napkin to absorb excess grease.
8. Serve with fry fish, escovitch fish, jerk chicken or pork or whatever your taste desires.

Serves 4-6
Enjoy!

Fried Dumplings (Johnny Cake)

<u>Ingredients:</u>

3/4 lbs sifted flour
¼ lbs sifted cornmeal
1 tsp baking powder
½ tsp salt
1 cup vegetable oil
1/3 cup milk
½ -1 cup ice cold water

<u>Method:</u>

1. Place the flour, baking powder and salt in a bowl.
2. Make a hole in the center of the mixture.
3. Add the milk and water knead into a dough. Continue kneading using the tips of the finger to knead until all the mixture is taken up, leaving the bowl clean.
4. Heat saucepan. Add vegetable oil and heat.
5. Break of small pieces of dough, ball size. Knead into a dumpling/ball shape, then use the ball of your hand – thumb side, to press lightly into the dough to make an indentation in the center.
6. Place in hot oil, lower flame and fry until golden brown.
7. Cover pot for approximately 2-3 minutes while frying to allow the dumplings to "soak"; that is to allow the flour/cornmeal to cook properly.
8. Place in bowl lined with a paper napkin to absorb excess grease.
9. Serve with fry fish, escovitch fish, jerk chicken or pork, ackee & salfish, or whatever your taste desires.

Serves 4-6
Enjoy!

Fried Dumplings (Johnny Cake)

Saltfish Fritters

<u>Ingredients:</u>

1 lbs sifted flour
¼ lbs sifted cornmeal
½ lbs salt fish
1 cup vegetable oil
1-2 seeds annoto (optional)
1 small onion sliced
1 sprig thyme or a dash of leaves
1 medium sized very red, ripe roma tomato
1 pinch hot pepper
1 dash black pepper
1 dash old bay seasoning

<u>Method:</u>

1. Place salt fish in a bowl with water to soak, preferably overnight.
2. Drain water off fish. Peal skin of fish and break into small pieces Approximately 1 cm in size.
3. Slice onion thinly, cut tomatoes and lay aside.
4. Place flour in a bowl. Add saltfish and all seasonings including powdered ones
5. Add a seed or two of annoto. Stir all ingredients together.
6. Make a hole in the center of the mixture. Pour approximately 1 cup of water in stirring and mixing simultaneously.
7. Mix to a running constituency that can be scooped up with a spoon.
8. Heat saucepan. Add vegetable oil and heat.
9. Scoop the mixture, spoon by spoon into the saucepan taking up the area of the saucepan.
10. Lower flame to medium, and allow fritters to fry until golden brown, paying attention to the edges which will slowly change color indicating it's time to flip fritters unto the opposite side to be fried. Use an egg lifter to flip.
11. Fry until golden brown, place on napkins on a platter and use a knife to separate or break up the fritter. Fritter can be separated where each fritter is joined as it as scooped into saucepan.
12. Continue until all fritter is fried, add more oil if necessary.
13. Serve alone or with eggs, bread, hot chocolate tea or whatever the taste.

Serves 8-12
Enjoy!

Fried Breadfruit

Ingredients:

1 roasted breadfruit
1 cup vegetable oil
2- 3 cups of water salted to taste

Method:

1. Cut breadfruit into two halves. Remove the heart. And peel breadfruit.
2. Slice breadfruit into ½-1 cm thick.
3. Pour water in bowl and add salt to taste. Place breadfruit slices in water to soak for approximately 1 -2 minutes.
4. Heat saucepan, add vegetable oil and heat. Do not pour all the oil in at once. Pour enough to allow food to fry.
5. Remove breadfruit from bowl, shake off excess water and carefully place in hot oil.
6. Fry to a quick light golden brown, turn unto other side fry and remove.
7. Place in plate lined with a paper napkin to absorb excess oil.
8. Serve with fry fish, escovitch fish, jerk chicken or pork or whatever your taste desires.

Serves 4-6
Enjoy!

Bammy

<u>Ingredients:</u>

1 pk bammy or 3-4 bammies
cup vegetable oil
1-2 cups milk

<u>Method:</u>

1. Cut bammy into 4 (four) quarters.
2. Pour milk in a bowl and place each piece of bammy into the milk to soak for approximately 2-3 minutes.
3. Heat saucepan, add oil and heat.
4. Remove bammy from milk. Shake off excess milk, place bammy carefully in hot oil and fry quickly to a light golden brown, turning from side to side.
5. Place in bowl lined with a paper napkin to absorb excess oil.
6. Serve with fry fish, escovitch fish, jerk chicken or pork or whatever your taste desires.

Serves 4-6
Enjoy!

Fried Plantains

<u>Ingredients:</u>

2-3 ripe plantains
1/3 cup vegetable oil

<u>Method:</u>

1. Cut both stems off plantains, and cut down one of the side seam.
2. Remove plantain from skin.
3. Cut in 3 sections of thirds.
4. Slice each third or section.
5. Heat saucepan, add vegetable oil, heat.
6. Add plantain slice and fry quickly until golden brown turning on each side.
7. Place in bowl lined with a paper napkin to absorb excess oil.
8. Serve with fry fish, escovitch fish, jerk chicken or pork or whatever your taste desires.

Serves 4-6
Enjoy!

Fried Green Bananas/Plantain

<u>Ingredients:</u>

2-3 green plantains or 6 green bananas
½ cup vegetable oil
Dash of salt
Dash of black pepper
Dash of lemon pepper

<u>Method:</u>

1. Cut both stems from plantains or green bananas and cut open one of the seams.
2. Cut plantain into thirds or banana in halves.
3. Slice each third plantain into thick slices approximately 0.5 cm thick.
4. Heat saucepan, add oil and heat.
5. Place plantain in oil and par fry. Remove, place in a crusher and squeeze flat, or use a fork to crush by pressing hard on plantain/banana.
6. Add a dash of black pepper, salt and lemon pepper. Rub it into the plantain.
7. Return plantain (banana) to hot oil and fry until golden brown turning from side to side.
8. Place in bowl lined with a paper napkin to absorb excess grease.
9. Serve with fry fish, escovitch fish, jerk chicken or pork or whatever your taste desires.

Serves 4-6
Enjoy!

Liver, Bacon, Onions & Green Bananas

Ingredients:
1 pk pre-packaged bacon (optional)
1-2 lbs liver
I onion
1-2 tomatoes
1 sprig thyme
1 clove garlic
2-tsp lime juice
1 tsp soy sauce
1 tbsp browning
1 tbsp ketchup
Pinch hot pepper
2 stalk eskellion
Dash black pepper
Dash dry seasonings
2-4 seeds crushed pimentos
¼ bell pepper (green)
½ tsp salt
1/3 cup vegetable oil

Method:
1. Clean liver by removing thin film/tissue off liver if present.
2. Cut liver into small 1 inch sizes.
3. Place in bowl, add lime juice and water. Rinse and drain.
4. Cut or chop onions, eskellion, tomatoes, garlic and add along with thyme
5. Add Browning, soy sauce, pepper, ad dry seasonings.
6. Use a gloved hand to rub seasoning into liver, cover and leave to marinate for approximately 20-30 minutes.
7. Open bacon, Remove strips. , place on a napkin to dry.
8. Heat saucepan. Place strips of bacon in pan and allow to fry. Stir. Do not allow bacon to burn.
9. Ensure that sufficient oil is in pot, approximately 1/3 cup.
10. Remove bacon, put aside. Or
11. Heat saucepan, add vegetable oil, heat
12. Pour bowl with all seasonings into bacon fat.
13. Add a little water in bowl, swish and pour in pot.
14. Stir, cover, lower flame and leave liver to cook and brown for Approximately 15-20 minutes until tender, stirring frequently.
15. Do not over-cook. Add bacon, add ketchup, dry seasonings. Stir.
16. Reseason, add some extra onion rings.
17. Turn off flame and serve with fried dumplings or your favorite side dish.
• Prepare green bananas according to recipe.

Serves 4-6, Enjoy!

Liver, Bacon, Onions & Green Bananas

Turn Cornmeal

Ingredients:

1 lbs red snapper fish (optional)
1 lbs corn meal
1 cup coconut milk (optional)
1 sprig thyme
2 stalks eskellion
2 tbsp sugar (optional)
Black pepper
½ tsp salt
dash dry seasoning
1 small pack green guango peas (pigeon) (optional)
1 clove garlic
1 tbsp butter
2-4 seeds pimentoes

Method:

1. Clean and prepare fish as to recipe of brown stew fish.
2. Rinse peas, add garlic and bring to boil.
3. Add coconut milk or butter. Allow coconut milk to cook for approximately 30 minutes.
4. Rinse eskellion and thyme and add to pot along with pimentos and dry seasoning and sugar.
5. Allow to cook for another 10 minutes, stir. Lower flame.
6. Measure cornmeal and add it slowly to mixture, cutting and folding as it is added. Stir. Corn meal should absorb all the mixture and be soft in dropping texture but not runny.
7. Cover and allow to steam on low flame for another 10-15 minutes until cornmeal is cooked.
8. Remove from flame stir and serve with fish.

Serves 4-6

Enjoy!

Steamed Callaloo

Ingredients:

1 bundle callaloo
¼ lbs saltfish (optional)
2-3 cooking tomatoes
1 onion
1 clove garlic
2-4seeds pimentos
1stalk eskellion
Black pepper
Dash dry seasonings
Pinch hot pepper
1/3 cup vegetale oil

Method:

1. Place saltfish in a bowl with ice cold water to soak to remove excess salt.
2. Drain water, remove skin from fish and break into small pieces.
3. Clean callaloo by stripping stem and removing wilted leaves and or seeds.
4. Chop or cut callaloo in 0.5 mm sizes, the smaller the better.
5. Pour about 2 tbsp vinegar in a bowl of water and callaloo. Rinse and drain.
6. Season callaloo. Add fish to calloo, cover with a plate and shake all seasonings together to distribute.
8. Allow to marinate for approx. 10 minutes.
9. Heat saucepan, add vegetable oil and heat.
10. Add callaloo, stir, cover, lower flame and allow to cook/steam for approximately 10-15 minuutes, or until tender stirring frequently. Callaloo will make its own gravy.
11. Do not over cook. Season to taste. Garnish with slices of onions or slices of hard boiled eggs. Serve with favorite side order.

Serves 4-6
Enjoy!

Steamed Callaloo

Pumpkin & Rice

Ingredients:

1 lbs pumpkin
2-3 pimento seeds
1 cup coconut milk (optional)
1-2 tbsp butter (optional)
1 sprig thyme
1 stalks eskellion
Dash black pepper
½ tsp salt
Dash powdered seasonings
1 cups rice (brown or white)

Method:

1. Peel pumpkin and cut in 1 inch cubes.
2. Place pot to boil with approximately 2 cups water.
3. Rinse pumpkin and add to pot.
4. Add coconut milk or butter, eskellion, thyme and pimento seeds, Stir, cover, lower flame and allow to cook for approximately 30 minutes. Pumpkin would become soft and tender.
5. Add salt, black pepper and dry seasonings to taste.
6. Measure 2 cups rice in a bowl, rinse, drain and add to pot. Stir.
7. Cover, lower flame and leave to cook until rice is dry and tender.
8. Stir. Remove from flame and serve.

Serves 4-6
Enjoy!

Seasoned Rice

Ingredients:

1/2 lbs pumpkin
2-3 pimento seeds
½ dozen ackees, cleaned
1/4 lbs salt fish
4-6 stalks callaloo (optional)
1 cup coconut milk (optional)
1-2 tbsp butter (optional)
½-2lbs chicken back or chicken (optional)
1 small bundle susumber (optional)
1 sprig thyme
1 stalks eskellion
Dash black pepper
*½ tsp salt if no salt fish is used. No additional salt is needed for salt fish.
Dash powdered seasonings
1 cups rice (brown or white)

Method:

1. Place salt fish in a bowl of water preferably overnight to soak. Drain water, remove fish skin and break up fish into small pieces. Set aside.
2. Clean ackees and cut each peg into two halves, and set aside.
3. Clean callaloo if used chop or cut in small pieces and set aside.
4. Clean chicken or chicken back by removing skin and or inside livers in chicken back. Chop in small 1 inch sizes, rinse in vinegar and season.
5. Heat saucepan and add chicken with season. Do not use any oil. Cover and allow chicken to brown/fry. Remove from flame and set aside.
6. Clean susumber by removing stems. Cut each cucumber in two halves, drain and set aside.
7. Peel pumpkin and cut in 1 inch cubes, rinse, drain and set aside.
8. Place pot to boil with approximately 3 cups water.
9. Add chicken/back, ackees, salt fish, susumber, callaloo, pumpkin coconut milk or butter, eskellion, thyme and pimento seeds, Stir, cover,
10. Lower flame and allow to cook for approximately 30 minutes.
11. Add black pepper and dry seasonings to taste.
12. Measure 2 cups rice in a bowl, , drain and add to pot. Stir.
13. Cover, lower flame and leave to cook until rice is dry and tender.
14. Stir. Remove from flame and serve.

Serves 4-6
Enjoy!

Seasoned Rice

Tin (Canned) Mackerel with Dumplings and Green Bananas

<u>Ingredients:</u>

1 can grace mackerel
1-2 cooking tomatoes
1 clove garlic
1 seeds pimentos
1 small onion
1 sprig thyme
1 stalks onion
1 pinch hot pepper
Black pepper
Dash dry powdered seasonings
1/3 cup vegetable oil
1 tbsp ketchup (optional)

<u>Method:</u>

1. Prepare dumpling and green bananas according to recipe.
2. Open canned mackerel and set aside.
3. Cut or chop seasonings and set aside.
4. Heat saucepan, add vegetable oil and heat.
5. Add seasonings, lower flame and stir, Cover for a minute or 2.
6. Add mackerel, stir, add black pepper and dash of powder seasoning to taste.
7. Add pimentos. Add 1 tbsp ketchup. Stir. Lower flame and allow to simmer for 5 minutes. Remove from flame and serve with your favorite side dish.

Serve 2-4
Enjoy!

Breakfast

Roast Breadfruit

<u>Ingredients:</u>

1 large roasting breadfruit (preferably yellow heart)

<u>Method:</u>

1. Use a sharp knife to cut the stem completely from the breadbruit.
2. Turn bread fruit onto stem and make a cross at the bottom. This allows for proper roasting of the insides of breadfruit.
3. Place on stove or heat oven to 350°F, place breadfruit on a baking sheet and bake until golden color.
4. If fruit is been done on stove top, turn the breadfruit unto another patch to roast as soon as you see the part directly on the flame roasted. Continue to turn the breadfruit from side to side until it is completed roasted.
5. Check the breadfruit to ensure that it is cook, by sticking a clean knife through it. The knife should come out clean without residue if cooked.
6. The knife test is the same for the oven or grilled roasted breadfruit.
7. Remove from fire, wrap in wet brown paper or kitchen towels.
8. Cut in two halves and peel.
9. Remove central heart, cut in slices approximately 1 inch thick.
10. Serve with callaloo or your favorite side dish.

Serves 6-8
Enjoy!

Chocolate Tea

Ingredients:

1-2 medium chocolates
1 piece nutmeg shell
1 cinnamon leaf
1 tbsp vanilla
1 dash cinnamon
1 dash all spice
1 pinch salt
1 dash nutmeg
small piece cinnamon stick (optional)
¼ cup evaporated milk (optional)
2 tbsp sweetened condensed milk (optional)
1/3 cup milk
1 cup sugar

Method:

1. Place chocolate in a pot. Add 2-3 cups water, cinnamon stick, leaf and nutmeg shell. Cover and boil.
2. Add remaining spices, lower flame and allow chocolate to boil until cook.
3. The chocolate will give off an aroma while cooking. An oil will form on the top as it cooks. Do not drain.
4. Add a cup or 2 of water while boiling.
5. Choclates should boil for 30-40 minutes to cook. You will know that it is cooked as it smells cooked.
6. Add one or two of your favourite milk.
7. Add sugar to taste.
8. Strain into your favorite tea pot and serve.

Enjoy!

Chocolate Tea

Scrambled Eggs

Ingredients:

2-4 eggs
¼ lbs salt fish (optional)
2 cooking tomatoes
1 stalk eskellion
1 onion
1 sprig thyme
Dash black pepper
Dash powered seasonings
2/3 cup vegetable oil
1/4 cup milk

Method:

1. Place salt fish in a bowl with cold water preferably overnight.
2. Drain water from fish, and remove skin from fish.
3. Break fish up in very small pieces, Set aside.
4. Break eggs in a clean bowl and whisk with a fork or egg whisker.
5. Cut all seasonings in a bowl.
6. Heat saucepan and add vegetable oil. Heat.
7. Lower flame, add seasonings from the bowl. Stir.
8. Add salt fish, stir and cover to simmer for 1-2 minutes.
9. Add milk to egg. Add mixture into saucepan. Stir.
10. Add a dash black pepper and powdered seasonings.
11. Stir mixture to mix all ingredients together. Cook for another 1-2 minutes.
12. Remove from flame and serve hot with fried dumplings bread, fried breadfruit or your favorite side order.

Serves 4-6
Enjoy!

Salads

Potato Salad

<u>Ingredients:</u>

2 lbs potatoes
1 stalk celery
1 stalked eskellion
1 small onion
Dash white pepper
2 eggs
4-6 tbsp mayonnaise
Dash black pepper
Dash old bay seasoning
¼ bell pepper (assorted colors)
1 pack mixed corn, carrots and green peas (optional)

<u>Method:</u>

1. Peel and dice potatoes add to sauce pot and bring to boil. Do not cover.
2. Place eggs in a small pot, cover and leave to boil for approx. 10 minutes.
3. Rinse celery and bell peppers in vinegar water. Drain. Chop finely. Put aside in a bowl.
4. Peel onion and eskellion. Chop finely. Add to bowl.
5. Remove eggs from flame. Rinse under cold water. Peel.
6. Chop finely. Add to bowl.
7. Check potatoes if cooked. Drain in a colander. Then run under cold tap water for 30 seconds. Drain and place in a large bowl.
8. Add mixed vegetables.
9. Add chopped egg and vegetables in bowl. Stir.
10. Add black pepper and old bay seasoning.
11. Add mayonnaise stir all ingredients together.
12. Chill and serve as a side order with your favorite dish.

Enjoy!

Macaroni Salad

Ingredients:

1 box shell macaroni
1 small pack shrimp (optional)
1 stalk celery
1 stalked eskellion
1 small onion
4-6 tbsp mayonnaise
Dash black pepper
Dash white pepper
Dash old bay seasoning
¼ bell pepper (assorted colors)
1 pack mixed corn, carrots and green peas
1 pinch salt

Method:

1. Place macaroni in a pot. Stir. Do not cover. Cook for approximately 10 minutes or until tender.
2. Rinse in cold water and drain.
3. Add to bowl.
4. Rinse celery and bell peppers in vinegar water. Drain. Chop finely. Put aside
5. Peel onion and eskellion. Chop finely.
6. Combine macaroni and chopped vegetables in a large bowl.
7. Add mixed vegetables.
9. Add black and white pepper along with old bay seasoning.
10. Add mayonnaise stir all ingredients together.
12. Chill and serve as a side order with your favorite dish.

Enjoy!

Macaroni Salad

Tossed Salad

<u>Ingredients:</u>

1 small hard green cabbage or
1 head lettuce
1 cucumber
2-4 roma tomatoes
½ bell peppers assorted
4-6 carrots
1-2 stalk celery
Salad Dressing

<u>Method:</u>

1. Place all vegetables in a large bowl. Cut cabbage in two halves. Add a little vinegar, add water, and drain.
2. Peel cucumber in a vertical fashion 1 cm in width. Peeling one section, leaving the other section unpeeled. Repeat this for a design.
3. Use the thong of a fork to make a vertical scallop, down the unpeeled side of the cucumber.
4. Cut in thin slices and lay aside.
5. Drain the cabbage, or lettuce. Place on a cutting board and shred or slice paper thin with a sharp knife.
6. Peel carrots with a vegetable peeler, shred on a 4-sided metal grater. Lay aside.
7. Arrange celery stalk and bell peppers. Slice or chop in thin slices.
8. Cut and deseed tomatoes. Cut each tomato in 4 quarters, leaving one whole.
9. Combine vegetables together and stir. Arrange in a salad bowl. Arrange the cucumbers along the edge of the bowl interlocking each other.
10. Cut the whole tomato. Open and deseed. Cut off the bottom to give it a firm base.
11. Cut in the shape of a flower, place in center of salad as garnish/decoration.
12. Add your favorite dressing.

Enjoy!

Tossed Salad

Juices

Soursop Juice

<u>Ingredients:</u>

1 ripe medium soursop
1 tin sweetened condensed milk
Dash vanilla
Dash almond
Dash ground cinnamon
Dash grated nutmeg
2-4 limes (optional). This replaces sweetened condensed milk.
½ -1 cup granulated sugar.

<u>Method:</u>

1. Rinse soursop and place in a bowl.
2. Gently peel off the skin. Discard of set aside to eat later.
3. Divide soursop into 2or 3 portions. Place each portion in a blender.
4. Add 2 cups water. Pulse or whip for approximately 1 minute to remove the soursop seeds.
5. Strain juice in a metal strainer. Or
6. Use a glove to juice soursop in a bowl. Strain juice in a metal strainer.
7. Add spices, add either lime juice or condensed milk, sweeten to taste.
8. Chill and serve

Serves 4-6
Enjoy!

Carrot Juice

Ingredients:

1 lbs carrot
½ lbs ginger
Dash vanilla
Dash cinnamon
Dash almond
Dash nutmeg
3-4 limes
1 can sweetened condensed milk (optional) This replaces ginger and limes.

Method:

1. Clean carrots and cut in small pieces.
2. Clean ginger and cut in small pieces.
3. Divide fruit into 2 or 3 portions. Place ginger and carrots together in blender with water.
4. Blend on high speed for 2-3 minutes until smooth.
5. Strain, Add spices, and sweeten to taste.
6. Chill and serve.

* PS DO NOT USE GINGER AND LIMES WITH SWEETENED CONDENSED MILK.

Serves 4-6
Enjoy!

Carrot & Beet Root Juice

<u>Ingredients:</u>

1 lbs carrot
¾ lbs beet or 2-3 medium beets
½ lbs ginger
Dash vanilla
Dash cinnamon
Dash almond
Dash nutmeg
3-4 limes
1 canned sweetened condensed milk (optional) This replaces ginger and limes.

<u>Method:</u>

1. Clean carrots and cut in small pieces.
2. Peel beet and cut in small pieces.
3. Clean ginger and cut in small pieces.
4. Combine vegetables, then divide into 2 or 3 portions. Place ginger, carrots and beets in blender with water.
5. Blend on high speed for 2-3 minutes until smooth.
6. Strain, Add spices, and sweeten to taste.
7. Chill and serve.

* PS DO NOT USE GINGER AND LIMES WITH SWEETENED CONDENSED MILK.

Serves 4-6
Enjoy!

Beet Root Juice

<u>Ingredients:</u>

1 lbs beets
½ lbs ginger
Dash vanilla
Dash cinnamon
Dash almond
Dash nutmeg
3-4 limes
1 can sweetened condensed milk (optional) This replaces ginger and limes.

<u>Method:</u>

1. Peel beetss and cut in small pieces.
2. Clean ginger and cut in small pieces.
3. Divide fruit into 2 or 3 portions. Place ginger and beets together in blender with water.
4. Blend on high speed for 2-3 minutes until smooth.
5. Strain, Add spices, and sweeten to taste.
6. Chill and serve.

* PS DO NOT USE GINGER AND LIMES WITH SWEETENED CONDENSED MILK.

Serves 4-6
Enjoy!

June Plum Juice

<u>Ingredients:</u>

1 dozen june plums (ripe or green)
½ lbs ginger
pinch
1 cup sugar
2-3 limes

<u>Method:</u>

1. Rinse june plums in a clean bowl. Drain water and peel.
2. Cut the flesh off the june plum to the seed. Discard seed.
3. Peel ginger and place in bowl with june plums.
4. Divide june plum and ginger into 2 or 3 portions to be blended.
5. Add 1 cup water to blender. Add june plum portion along with 1-2 cups of water to fill blender.
6. Blend on high smooth until smooth for 1-3 minutes.
7. Strain, add spice. Sweeten to taste.
8. Chill and serve.

Serves 4-6
Enjoy!

Cucumber Juice

<u>Ingredients:</u>

2-3 large cucumbers
½ lbs ginger
1 cup sugar
1 bottle (1 pt) ginger ale
2-3 limes

<u>Method:</u>

1. Rinse cucumbers and cut in small pieces in a bowl.
2. Peel ginger and cut in small pieces.
3. Add 1 cup water to blender. Divide cucumber into 2 portions.
4. Add each portion to blender, then add water to fill.
5. Blend on high speed for 2-3 minutes until smooth.
6. Strain, Sweeten to taste.
7. Add lime juice.
8. Open ginger ale and pour into cucumber juice to "chase and flavor."
9. Chill and serve.

Serves 4-6
Enjoy!

Cucumber & Melon Drink

<u>Ingredients:</u>

2-3 large cucumbers
2-3 lbs melon or ½ small melon
½ lbs ginger
1 cup sugar
1 bottle (1 pt) ginger ale
2-3 limes

<u>Method:</u>

1. Rinse cucumbers and cut in small pieces in a bowl.
2. Scoop or ball melon completely out of skin.
3. Peel ginger and cut in small pieces.
4. Combine melon, cucumber and ginger in a bowl.
5. Add 1 cup water to blender. Divide fruits into measurable portions.
4. Add each portion to blender, add water to fill.
5. Blend on high speed for 2-3 minutes until smooth.
6. Add lime juice.
7. Strain, Sweeten to taste.
8. Chill and serve.

Serves 4-6
Enjoy!

Ginger Ale

Ingredients:

1-2 lbs ginger
1 -1/2 cup sugar
1 bottle (1 pt) ginger ale

Method:

1. Rinse ginger. strip or peel skin.
2. Cut ginger in small pieces and place in a bowl.
3. Add 1 cup water to blender. Divide ginger into blender portions.
4. Add each portion to blender, add water to fill.
5. Blend on high speed for 2-3 minutes until smooth.
6. Strain, Sweeten to taste.
7. Open ginger ale and pour into juice to "chase and flavor."
8. Chill and serve.

Serves 4-6
Enjoy!

Passion Fruit

Ingredients:

6-12 ripe passion fruit
¼ lb ginger
4-6 limes
Sugar to taste

Method:

1. Rinse fruits, cut open, and remove inside, set aside.
2. Rinse ginger, chop and set aside.
3. Combine passion and ginger into blender and blend on low speed.
4. Strain into a bowl.
5. Add lime juice.
6. Sweeten to taste.
7. Chill and serve.

Enjoy.

Papaya Juice

Ingredients:

1 ripe papaya
¼ lb ginger
 4-6 limes
Sugar to taste

Method:

1. Cut papaya open in two halves
2. Remove the seeds and discard
3. Peel the papaya and cut into small pieces
4. Add to blender along with water and ginger
5. Blend until smooth
6. Strain and sweeten to taste
7. Chill and serve.

Enjoy!

Fruit Punch

<u>Ingredients:</u>

1-2 apples
1 banana
2-4 june plums
1 large ripe mango. Do not peel.
1-2 slices pineapple
½ lbs papaya
¼ lb ginger
2-3 limes
Sugar

<u>Method:</u>

1. Rinse fruits and cut into small 1 inch sizes. Remove the seeds.
2. Rinse ginger, cut in small pieces and add to fruits.
3. Place approx. 2 cups of water in blender, add fruit in small portions.
4. Cover and blend on high speed until smooth
5. Strain through a sieve to desired consistency.
6. Add lime juice and sugar to taste.
7. Chill and serve

Enjoy!

Pineapple Juice

Ingredients:

1 medium size pineapple (preferably sugar loaf type) or
1 can chunky pineapple
¼ lbs ginger
1-2 limes
Sugar to taste

Method:

1. Peel pineapple clean of all skin. Place the skin aside in a pot.
2. Cut pineapple into chunks. Scrape skin from ginger, cut in small pieces and add to pineapple. Or
3. Open can of pineapple chunks, add to prepared ginger, add 1-2 cups water to blender and blend until smooth. or
4. Add 1-2 cups water to blender, add pineapple and ginger and blend until smooth.
5. Strain in a fine sieve, add lime juice to flavor
6. Sweeten to taste.
7. Chill and serve.

*USING PINEAPPLE SKIN TO MAKE JUICE.

1. Add 3-4 cups of water to a pot and bring to boil.
2. Add pineapple skin to pot. Scrape ginger, crush gently and add to pot.
3. Cover pot. Turn off flame. Leave to brew for approximately 1-2 hours.
4. Strain in a sieve, add lime juice to flavor, and sugar to taste.
5. Chill and serve or mix with juice made from pineapple. Stir and serve.

Enjoy!

Snacks

Coconut or Cut Cake

<u>Ingredients:</u>

1 dry coconut
½ - ¾ lb. dark sugar
½ lb. ginger
Aluminum foil or banana leaves for drying
Dash of cinnamon

<u>Method:</u>

1. Break the coconut and husk it.
2. Rinse coconut and cut in small piece approximately 0.5 mm sizes.
3. Peel ginger and shred or cut in small sizes as coconut.
4. Add coconut, ginger sugar to a sauce pot. Add approx.2-3 cups water.
5. Add cinnamon.
6. Stir, cover, lower flame and leave to cook until thicken. The mixture should come together forming a caramel with a thick dropping consistency.
7. Turn off flame, spread aluminum foil to desired size or banana leaves on a plate, board or counter top.
8. Use a large spoon to scoop mixture unto foil or leaf in separate and individual heaps.
9. Allow to cool at room temperature.
10. Serve as a snack or just a delicacy to munch on!

Enjoy!

Coconut Grated Cake

Ingredients:

1 dry coconut
½ - ¾ lb. dark sugar
½ lb. ginger
Aluminum foil or banana leaves for drying
Dash of cinnamon

Method:

1. Break the coconut and husk it.
2. Rinse coconut and ginger. Cut in small pieces, add to blender with a very small amount of water and grate; or grate with a metal grater.
3. Remove from blender.
4. Add coconut, ginger sugar to a sauce pot. Add approx.2-3 cups water.
5. Add cinnamon.
6. Stir, cover, lower flame and leave to cook until thicken. The mixture should come together forming a caramel with a thick dropping consistency.
7. Turn off flame, spread aluminum foil to desired size or banana leaves on a plate, board or counter top.
8. Use a large spoon to scoop mixture unto foil or leaf in separate and individual heaps.
9. Allow to cool at room temperature.
10. Serve as a snack or just a delicacy to munch on!

Enjoy!

Rock Bun

Ingredients:

1 egg slightly beaten and set aside
½ lb. flour
2 ½ level tsp. baking powder
¼ lbs. sugar
¼ level tsp. salt
¼ lb. raisin
¼ lb. margarine
Dash nutmeg
2 tsp vanilla
Dash ground cinnamon
1/3 cup milk

Method:

1. Preheat the oven at 375°F
2. Sieve together flour and baking powder.
3. Add the sugar. This speeds up the rubbing in of the butter.
4. Add the butter. Use a pastry blender to cut the butter into the mixture aerating the flour at the same time.
5. Use the tips of your finger to aerate the flour mixture until it becomes like bread crumbs on your finger tips.
6. Add the fruit. (raisins)
7. Beat the egg and mix it with other liquid ingredients.
8. Make a hole into the flour. Pour in the liquid ingredients, mixing the whole mixture smoothly to a thick dropping constituency.
9. Spoon unto a baking sheet and bake to a light golden brown or until toothpick comes out clean on testing

**" Rock refers to the rough shape, not the texture of the bun."

Serves 4-6

Enjoy!

Sweet Potato Pudding

<u>Ingredients:</u>

1-2 lbs sweet potato
2 tbsp flour
½ lbs. raisin
1 cup coconut milk (sweetened)
2 cup milk (sweetened)
1 tbsp. butter
1 tsp. vanilla
1 tsp. almond
1 tsp. ground cinnamon
1b tsp. nutmeg
1 tsp. all spice

<u>Method:</u>

1. Heat oven to 375°.
2. Peel sweet potatoes and grate, or cut in small pieces and process in food processor.
3. Add potatoes to a bowl. Add flour and spices along with the raisins. Make a hole in the center of the mixture.
4. Add the liquid mixing and stirring simultaneously, The mixture should have a thick running constituency.
5. Pour into a baking dish.
6. Bake for the first 45 minutes then lower to 250° and continue to bake until cook.
7. The top of the pudding should be moist with a little cream or liquid on the top when fully cooked.
8. Test with a toothpick, or knife. Whatever is used to test should be pulled out clean when pudding is baked.
9. Cool and serve.

Enjoy!

Cornmeal Pudding

Ingredients:

1 lb. cornmeal
2 tbsp flour
½ lbs. raisin
1 cup coconut milk (sweetened)
2 cup milk (sweetened)
1 tbsp. butter
1 tsp. vanilla
1 tsp. almond
1 tsp. ground cinnamon
1b tsp. nutmeg
1 tsp. all spice

Method:

1. Heat oven to 375°.
2. Sieve cornmeal, flour in a bowl. Add spices and raisins. Make a hole in the center of the mixture.
3. Add the liquid mixing and stirring simultaneously. The mixture should have a thick running constituency.
4. Pour into a baking dish.
5. Bake for the first 45 minutes then lower to 250° and continue to bake until cook.
6. The top of the pudding should be moist with a little cream or liquid on the top when fully cooked.
7. Test with a toothpick, or knife. Whatever is used to test should be pulled out clean when pudding is baked.
8. Cool and serve.

Enjoy!

Bread Pudding

Ingredients:

1 loaf of dry stale sliced bread
2-3 cup. of sweetened milk sweetened with sugar
¼-1/2 lbs butter
¼ lb. raisin
Dash of nutmeg
Dash of ground cinnamon
Dash of vanilla
Dash of almond
Dash of all spice
2-3 tbsp white rum (optional)

Method:

1. Butter each slice of bread double-sided. Cut each slice into small cubes.
2. Place in a bowl. Add raisins and spices.
3. Add sweetened milk enough to saturate the bread.
4. Add rum, and mix and stir all ingredients together.
5. Set mixture aside for approximately 30 minutes, allowing the bread to soak and break up.
6. Heat oven to 375°F.
7. Use a whisker or hand mixer (on slow speed) to completely break up the bread.
8. Pour in mixing bowl and bake for approximately 45 minutes. Lower flame and bake for another 15 or 20 minutes or until tooth pick or knife is clean when pudding is tested.
9. Cool and serve.

Enjoy!

Christmas Cake / Wedding Cake Or (Black Cake)

<u>Ingredients:</u>

10 oz. flour
1 level tsp. baking powder
1 cup milk (optional)
8 oz. sugar
8 oz. butter
1 bottle browning
4-5 eggs
Grated rind of 1 lemon/lime
2 tbsp powdered chocolate (optional)
1 nutmeg grated
2 cups white rum
2 cup port or fruit wine
2 tbsp powdered cinnamon
2 tbsp allspice
2 tbsp vanilla
2 tbsp almond (liquid)
2 tbsp rosewater
1 lb raisinb
2 oz. ground or chopped almonds or unsalted peanuts
1 lb currants
1 lb mixed peel
¼ lbs prunes (optional)
2 tbsp black molasses (optional)
Wooden spoon
Electric mixer

<u>Method:</u>

1. Preferably overnight, place dried fruits, (that is raisins, currants, mixed peel and prunes) into a pot. Add 1 cup wine and 1 cup rum, stir. Lower flame to low, cover and allow fruits to steam for approximately 20-30 minutes. Remove from flame and allow to cool.
2. Preheat oven at 375°. Sieve flour and baking powder in a bowl. Stir to incorpo rate air, cover and put aside.
3. Place butter and sugar in electric mixer. Turn thermostat to cream and leave it to cream, checking on it frequently and using a spatula to clean the sides of the mixer. Cream until wavy or foamy. Turn off mixer.
4. Place steamed fruit in a food processor and chop finely.
5. Grate nutmeg and place aside,
6. Grate lime or lemon and place aside.

7. Grease and flour baking pans and set aside.
8. Break each egg in a small bowl. Remove the eye.
9. Transfer eggs to a bowl and beat slightly with a whisker.
10. Transfer contents of mixer into a large bucket or bowl.
11. Pour in the amount of 1 egg at a time into the large bowl. Use the wooden spoon to mix and stir the egg into the creamed mixture. Do not pour too much egg at a time as the mixture will cradle. (If cradling occurs; don't panic, just keep stirring vigourously until it is mixed out). Continue beating the egg in until finish.
12. Add all the spices including nutmeg and lemon/lime rind and stir.
13. Add all the steamed fruits and molasses. Stir.
14. Add chocolate and chopped nuts and stir
15. Add the browning and stir. It is safe to add the whole bottle of browning. The color is dependent on the individual and the strength of the browning.
16. Add the remaining rum and wine. Stir. (According to individual's taste)
17. Add the flour mixture in portions. Cutting, folding and mixing simultaneously with the wooden spoon to incorporate air and the flour into the mixture.
18. Repeat action until all the flour is folded in. The mixture should now be of thick dropping constituency.
19. Place a pot, metal bowl or baking pan ½-3/4 filled with water on the oven shelf below the shelf the cake will be baked on. This allows for steam to be present in the oven.
20. Pour into 2 or 3 greased baking pan. Clean the pans of all spills on top edge and outside of pans. These spills burn first on a cake.
21. Bake at 375°F on second shelf of oven for approximately 1 hr. Check cake. Do not slam over door. This will cause cake to crack or sink.
22. Lower flame slowly, to 300°F allowing cake to continue to bake. (Changing the temperature rapidly will cause cake to flop in the center).
23. Check cake if baked. Knife or toothpick should be pulled out clean when baked.
24. Turn off oven and remove cake. Leaving cake in oven will dry it out even though oven is off.
25. Allow cake to cool, wet with wine to moisten and keep.
26. Slice and serve or icing after a day or two depending on the purpose – birthday or wedding cake.

Enjoy!

Pineapple Up-Side Down Cake

<u>Ingredients:</u>

2 pack plain cake mix
1 large can pineapple slices
8 ozs, sugar
6 eggs
2 cups milk
1-2 cups vegetable oil
1 small bottle maraschino cherries

<u>Method:</u>

1. Heat oven to 375°F. Grease and flour a rectangular baking pan or casserole dish.
2. Prepare cake mix according to directions on package.
3. Spread sugar on the base of baking pan, lightly over the entire surface.
4. Open pineapple, drain juice and arrange slices on top of the sugar, enough to cover the entire area of the baking pan.
5. Place a cherry inside the circle of each pineapple slice.
6. Pour the cake mixture slowly on top of the pineapples.
7. Wipe off any spills on the edge or outside of the cake.
8. Bake on the second shelf for 30-45 minutes until baked.
9. Check cake if bake, knife or pick should come out clean when baked.
10. Cool cake and turn it carefully out of the baking pan down side up.
11. Cool slice and serve.

Enjoy!

Porridge
Or Hot Cereals

Cornmeal Porridge

<u>Ingredients:</u>

½ lbs cornmeal
1/3 cup milk
1/3 cup dry powdered milk (optional)
½ cup sugar
1/3 cup evaporated milk (optional)
2-3 tbsp sweetened condensed milk (optional)
¼ cup coconut milk (optional)
Dash cinnamon
Dash nutmeg
Dash vanilla
Dash all spice
1-2 tsp vanilla
1 cinnamon leave or stick
¼ tsp salt.

<u>Method:</u>

1. Place pot on stove with 2-3 cups water to boil.
2. Add all spices.
3. Measure cornmeal and put aside in a bowl.
4. As the water begins to boil, add a cup of cold water to cornmeal and mix to a smooth paste.
5. Pour the cornmeal into the water stirring the pot as the cornmeal is poured in to prevent lumps.
6. Add a little cold water to cornmeal bowl, swiss it around to remove all its contents. Continue stirring as the pot boils.
7. Add coconut milk. Stir.
8. Check constituency of the porridge as it starts boiling. It should not be too thick "popping" at the beginning as it will get thicker as it boils, and this prevents proper cooking. If too thick add water slowly while stirring to a smooth consistency. Stir.
8. Lower flame, do not cover. Allow porridge to boil for 20-30 minutes until the aroma of cooked cornmeal fills the air.
9. Mix powder milk with 1/4 cup water, mix to a smooth paste and add to porridge.
10. Bring to a boil, add whichever milk is desired, sweeten to taste.
11. Add a dash of nutmeg and cinnamon. Stir.
12. Serve hot or as desired.

Serves 4-6
Enjoy!

Cream of Wheat Porridge

<u>Ingredients:</u>

1 cup cream of wheat
1/3 cup milk
1/3 cup dry powdered milk (optional)
½ cup sugar
1/3 cup evaporated milk (optional)
2-3 tbsp sweetened condensed milk (optional)
Dash cinnamon
Dash nutmeg
Dash vanilla
Dash all spice
1-2 tsp vanilla
1 cinnamon leave or stick
¼ tsp salt.

<u>Method:</u>

1. Place pot on stove with 2 cups water to boil.
2. Add all spices.
3. Measure cream of wheat and put aside in a bowl.
4. As the water begins to boil, add a cup of cold water to cream of wheat and mix to smooth paste.
5. Pour the cream of wheat mixture into the water stirring the pot simultaneously to prevent lumps.
6. Add a little cold water to bowl, swiss it around to remove all its contents. Continue stirring as the pot boils.
7. Check constituency of the porridge as it starts boiling. It should not be too thick "popping" at the beginning as it will get thicker as it boils, and this prevents proper cooking. If too thick add water slowly while stirring to a smooth consistency. Stir.
8. Lower flame, do not cover. Porridge cooks in 5-7 minutes.
9. Mix powder milk with1/4 cup water, mix to a smooth paste and add to porridge.
10. Bring to a boil, add whichever milk is desired, sweeten to taste.
11. Add a dash of nutmeg and cinnamon. Stir.
12. Serve hot or at desired temperature.

Serves 4-6
Enjoy!

Oats Porridge

<u>Ingredients:</u>

1-2 cups oats
1/3 cup milk
1/3 cup dry powdered milk (optional)
½ cup sugar
1/3 cup evaporated milk (optional)
2-3 tbsp sweetened condensed milk (optional)
Dash cinnamon
Dash nutmeg
Dash vanilla
Dash all spice
1-2 tsp vanilla
1 cinnamon leave or stick
¼ tsp salt.

<u>Method:</u>

1. Place pot on stove with 2-3 cups water to boil.
2. Add all spices.
3. Measure oats and put aside in a bowl.
4. As the water begins to boil, add a cup of cold water to oats and mix.
5. Pour the oats into the water stirring the pot simultaneously to prevent lumps. Stir.
6. Continue stirring as the pot boils.
7. Check constituency of the porridge as it starts boiling. It should not be too thick "popping" at the beginning as it will get thicker as it boils. If too thick add water slowly while stirring to a smooth consistency. Stir.
8. Lower flame, do not cover. Porridge cooks in 5 minutes.
9. Mix powder milk with1/4 cup water, mix to a smooth paste and add to porridge.
10. Bring to a boil, add whichever milk is desired, sweeten to taste.
11. Add a dash of nutmeg and cinnamon. Stir.
12. Serve hot or at desired temperature.

Serves 4-6
Enjoy!

Plantain Porridge

<u>Ingredients:</u>

2 green plantains or partially ripe plantains
1/3 cup milk
1/3 cup dry powdered milk (optional)
½ cup sugar
1/3 cup evaporated milk (optional)
2-3 tbsp sweetened condensed milk (optional)
Dash cinnamon
Dash nutmeg
Dash vanilla
Dash all spice
1-2 tsp vanilla
1 cinnamon leave or stick
¼ tsp salt.

<u>Method:</u>

1. Place pot on stove with 2-3 cups water to boil.
2. Add all spices.
3. Cut off the top and bottom stem of the plantain. Make a slit down one of the seam to make for easier peeling.
4. As the water begins to boil, peel the plantains, scrape the plantain clean of all skin. Cut into 2 or 3 portions.
5. Place in blender, add 1 cup boiling water from pot to blender. Blend until smooth.
6. Pour contents of blender into pot. Stir.
7. Lower flame, do not cover. Porridge cooks in 5-7 minutes. Savor the aroma. You will know it's cooked.
8. Mix powder milk with1/4 cup water, mix to a smooth paste and add to porridge.
9. Bring to a boil, add whichever milk is desired, sweeten to taste.
10. Add a dash of nutmeg and cinnamon. Stir.
11. Serve hot or as desired.

Serves 4-6
Enjoy!

Green Banana Porridge

Ingredients:

½ dozen green bananas
1/3 cup milk
1/3 cup dry powdered milk (optional
½ cup sugar
1/3 cup evaporated milk (optional)
2-3 tbsp sweetened condensed milk (optional)
Dash cinnamon
Dash nutmeg
Dash vanilla
Dash all spice
1-2 tsp vanilla
1 cinnamon leave or stick
¼ tsp salt.

Method:

1. Place pot on stove with 2-4 cups water to boil.
2. Add all spices.
3. Cut of the top and bottom stem. Make a slit down one of the seam to make for easier peeling. Peel and scrape of all skin. Or
4. Rinse banana, remove stems and cut each unpeeled banana into 2 or 3 pieces.
5. Separate into portions to blend. Add 1-2 cups boiling water into blender.
6. Add bananas. Blend until smooth.
7. Pour contents of blender into pot. Stir.
8. Lower flame, do not cover. Porridge cooks in 5-7 minutes. Savor the aroma. You will know it's cooked.
9. Mix powder milk with1/4 cup water, mix to a smooth paste and add to porridge.
10. Bring to a boil, add whichever milk is desired, sweeten to taste.
11. Add a dash of nutmeg and cinnamon. Stir.
12. Serve hot or as desired.

Serves 4-6
Enjoy!

Rice Porridge

Ingredients:

1 lb rice
1/3 cup milk
1/3 cup dry powdered milk (optional)
½ cup sugar
1/3 cup evaporated milk (optional)
2-3 tbsp sweetened condensed milk (optional)
Dash cinnamon
Dash nutmeg
Dash vanilla
Dash all spice
1-2 tsp vanilla
1 cinnamon leave or stick
¼ tsp salt.

Method:

1. Place pot on stove with 2-3 cups water to boil.
2. Add all spices.
3. Place rice in a bowl. Rinse and add to pot, stir or add pre-cooked rice to bowl, mix with a little water and add to pot. Stir.
4. Lower flame and leave to cook. Do not cover. Stir frequently to prevent sticking and clumping.
5. Add extra water if necessary.
6. Cook until rice is soft, tender and thickening.
7. Mix powder milk with1/4 cup water, mix to a smooth paste and add to porridge.
8. Bring to a boil, add whichever milk is desired, sweeten to taste.
9. Add a dash of nutmeg and cinnamon. Stir.
10. Serve hot or as desired.

Serves 4-6
Enjoy!

Bulga Porridge

<u>Ingredients:</u>

2 cups bulga
1/3 cup milk
1/3 cup dry powdered milk (optional)
½ cup sugar
1/3 cup evaporated milk (optional)
2-3 tbsp sweetened condensed milk (optional)
Dash cinnamon
Dash nutmeg
Dash vanilla
Dash all spice
1-2 tsp vanilla
1 cinnamon leave or stick
¼ tsp salt.

<u>Method:</u>

1. Place bulga in a bowl. Add 2-3 cups cold water and leave to soak (preferably overnight). Bulga should absorb all or most of the water and swell.
2. Place pot on stove with 3-4 cups water to boil.
3. Add all spices.
4. Add bulga to pot and stir.
5. Lower flame, do not cover. Allow bulga to cook until soft, tender and thickening.
6. Stir porridge frequently to prevent sticking and clumping.
7. Add water if necessary.
8. Mix powder milk with1/4 cup water, mix to a smooth paste and add to porridge.
9. Bring to a boil, add whichever milk is desired, sweeten to taste.
10. Add a dash of nutmeg and cinnamon. Stir.
11. Serve hot or as desired.

Serves 4-6
Enjoy!

Hominy Corn Porridge

Ingredients:

2 pack hominy corn
1/3 cup milk
1/3 cup dry powdered milk (optional)
½ cup sugar
1/3 cup evaporated milk (optional)
2-3 tbsp sweetened condensed milk (optional)
Dash cinnamon
Dash nutmeg
Dash vanilla
Dash all spice
1-2 tsp vanilla
1 cinnamon leave or stick
¼ tsp salt.

Method:

1. Place hominy corn in a bowl or the pot it will be cooked in. Add water, and drain.
2. Add 2-3 cups cold water, or just enough to cover the corn. Cover and leave to soak (preferably overnight). Corn should absorb all or most of the water and swell.
3. Place pot on stove with 3-4 cups water to boil.
4. Add all spices.
5. Add hominy corn to pot and stir.
6. Lower flame, do not cover. Allow porridge to cook until hominy is tender and thickening.
7. Stir porridge frequently to prevent sticking and clumping.
8. Add water if necessary.
9. Mix powder milk with1/4 cup water, mix to a smooth paste and add to porridge.
10. Bring to a boil, add whichever milk is desired, sweeten to taste.
11. Add a dash of nutmeg and cinnamon. Stir.
12. Serve hot or as desired.

Serves 4-6
Enjoy!

"How To"- Tid Bits

1.   The rice is dried but the grains are hard.

Ans.   Lower flame, very low. Wet aluminum foil or plastic wrap and place on top of rice. Cover and allow to steam for approximately 10-15 minutes.

2.   The rice burned while cooking.

Ans.   Rinse a piece of celery, green tomato or a piece of green cucumber. Stick it in the center of rice and Cover. This can be done for soup or gravy. I personally prefer a piece of celery.

3.   The food is salt.

Ans.   Celery is great or a green tomato. Just rinse, place in food, cover and leave for a few minutes.

4.   Cooking rice. Not sure when enough water is in the pot.

Ans.   This suggestion comes from my deceased grandmother, but has been tried and proven over and over again.

Stand a fork in the rice after adding the water, salt etc after stirring. If the fork stands on its own, it has the correct amount of water. If the fork falls over, the pot has in too much water or too little rice.

5.   Cooking dried kidney beans. Pressed for time, the beans were not soaked.

Ans.   Rinse beans, add garlic and just enough water to barely cover the peas or beans. Bring to a quick boil. Sink the beans, by adding 1-2 cups cold water. Then allow to cook. The process of 'sinking' helps to soften the beans/peas.

6.   Gravy is thin, needs to be thickened.

Ans.   Combine 1-2 teaspoon cornstarch with approximately 3 tablespoons water. Stir. Add to gravy
or
Peel a small irish potato. Dice in small pieces. Add to gravy and allow to cook and thicken.
Or
Grate a piece of toast and add to gravy.

7.   Cooking meat or chicken. Pressed for time, no time to prep or marinate meat/chicken.

Ans.   Grate onion, 2 cloves garlic and a piece of ginger unto meat. Make sure the juices from these are not wasted, but added to the meat. Add all other seasonings. Rub seasonings into meat and cook.

CPSIA information can be obtained
at www.ICGtesting.com
Printed in the USA
246579LV00002B